MISO

First published in the United Kingdom in 2016 under the title *Miso Tasty* by Pavilion

This revised and updated edition first published in the UK by Pavilion
An imprint of HarperCollins*Publishers* 2026

An imprint of HarperCollins*Publishers* Ltd
1 London Bridge Street
London SE1 9GF

www.harpercollins.co.uk

HarperCollinsPublishers
Macken House
39/40 Mayor Street Upper
Dublin 1
D01 C9W8
Ireland

10 9 8 7 6 5 4 3 2 1

ISBN 9780008739508

Publishing Director: Laura Russell
Commissioning Editor: Lucy Smith
Editorial Assistant: Daisy Gudmunsen
Design Manager: Alice Kennedy-Owen
Layout Designer: Kei Ishimaru
Photographer: Yuki Sugiura
Food and Prop Stylist: Aya Nishimura
Illustrator: Clare Owen
Copyeditor: Lucy Bannell
Production Controller: Grace O'Byrne
Proofreader: Sarah Epton
Indexer: Vanessa Bird

Printed and bound in China

WHEN USING KITCHEN APPLIANCES PLEASE ALWAYS FOLLOW THE MANUFACTURER'S INSTRUCTIONS

For more information visit:
www.harpercollins.co.uk/green

MISO

From Japanese Classics
to Everyday Umami

BONNIE
CHUNG

PAVILION

味噌鐵
カギロイ
美味ニシテ滋養
東京 神田 神保町

CONTENTS

味噌漬
万久特製

FOREWORD TO THE 2026 EDITION

It has been a cathartic – almost indulgent – journey to review and refresh this book, ten years after its first publication. Looking back, my obsession with miso was ahead of its time, so I must express my thanks to my publishers, who backed my passion from day one. Thankfully, and to my own surprise sometimes, my enthusiasm for miso has not waned over the last decade. If anything, it has grown stronger.

When I started my business, Miso Tasty, 15 years ago, it was hard. It took us three years to develop our first batch for sale and, even then, miso was too often dismissed as a niche ingredient; nobody really knew what it was, apart from that it went into Japanese miso soup... To think that, more than a decade on, I am still writing about miso and that Miso Tasty has become a global brand – so my creations are enjoyed around the world – is WILD!

I have loved the opportunity to build on my original cookbook. This time, I've included more about both the fermentation process and the sensory science behind the magic of miso. I've also introduced new chapters to reflect how miso's story has moved on, and, indeed, how I have, with ten years more experience under my belt.

I don't see myself as a miso expert, more as a student and advocate of miso. I am in awe of the real experts in Japan, who have dedicated their whole lives (and often their entire families) to miso-making. In recent years, I have also developed a deep respect for innovative miso-makers outside Japan, who are pioneering miso in exciting ways I never dreamed of, always with sustainability at the forefront. I'll be introducing a number of these trailblazers to you – they are the future of miso – in the pages that follow.

The new chapter I am particularly excited for you to read is The Secret Weapon. It reveals all the everyday ways in which miso can supercharge your existing repertoire of dishes. This stealthy approach to cooking with miso has been the single most transformative tip I have been teaching to home cooks over the last decade and more. I have realized that our best dishes tend not to be the fancy food we make on high days and holidays, but actually those recipes we repeat on a weeknight because we crave them, because we know they always work, because everyone likes them and because they're quick and economical. I have loaded this book full of dishes just like that, elevated by a touch of miso, and I can't wait for you to try them!

A lot has changed over the last ten years. Miso is now available everywhere, not just – as it was back then – in health or Asian speciality shops. It is featured on TV shows, on restaurant menus and in cookbooks, as a regular part of non-Japanese dishes. Yet, still, for many home cooks, miso remains a mystery. I hope that this book, and my work, continues to bring many more cooks into the fold of miso and its superpowers, so that one day a jar (or two) of miso will be in every kitchen, bringing natural, nutritious flavours to all our food.

Bonnie x

最上醤油
三社祭
香吟 1K 880円
小雪 1K 910円
仙台粒 1K 830円
吹雪 1K 980円

INTRODUCTION

Miso can and should play a vital role in your kitchen, lying quiet in its jar like a sleeping ninja, ready to add instant depth, texture and nutrition. Whether you want to recreate a dish you loved in a Japanese restaurant, or you want to experiment, or simply add more flavour to your cooking – even your desserts – miso has got you covered.

For me, writing about miso is like describing an old friend. I know her intimately, this favourite ingredient of mine, both her impressive qualities *and* her frustrating foibles. This is a truthful book: I will wax lyrical about miso, but I will also point out where she is not perfect and show you how to avoid common pitfalls when cooking with her.

I have poured everything I have learned over the last 15 years into these pages, because I want this to be *the* ultimate and timeless guide to miso. I have included meticulous tips on how to nail every recipe every time, since sometimes success in the kitchen is as much about technique as it is about having the best ingredients.

What makes this book special, though, is that I don't just show you *what* to cook with miso by means of a bunch of recipes. Instead, I teach you *how* to cook with miso. The distinction is important. I don't want you to simply follow a recipe, instead I want you to learn to cook with miso intuitively; this requires a deeper understanding of the ingredient, which I am uniquely placed to share with you.

This book is divided into four chapters, representing each of the roles miso can play in your kitchen. The Quintessential Japanese Ingredient is all about conquering the classics, such as miso soup, ramen, miso cod and miso aubergines. The Flavour Partner will show you how to have fun with miso, by pairing it with reliable buddies. In that chapter, I'll teach you how to make endless tasty dressings and sauces intuitively, with just a couple of store cupboard ingredients.

In The Secret Weapon, I reveal to you my formula for supercharging your existing repertoire of dishes. In these recipes, miso is the transformer and flavour pusher, a discreet friend who will help you in the kitchen every day. The last chapter, The Dessert Twist, is a collection of show-stopping puddings upgraded with that salty-caramel miso flavour hit, giving a surprisingly moreish savoury edge to cakes, ice cream, brownies and more.

I hope this book will inspire you to enjoy miso in your kitchen all the time, as well as help you ultimately become a miso advocate yourself. If, one day, you find yourself grabbing a jar of miso to flavour up your cooking without referencing this book, my work here is done!

Wishing you a lifetime of flavourful, umami-rich cooking.

WHAT IS MISO?

Miso is quite unlike anything else, though I realize that's not the answer to the question! I can, though, say it with authority. After 15 years championing this single ingredient, I have not discovered anything to rival miso's superpowers in my kitchen.

Essentially, miso is a fermented soya bean paste made with a grain – such as rice or barley – salt, water and a bacterial culture called *Aspergillus oryzae*. Though the ingredients are simple, the transformation they undergo is extraordinary.

As with other fermented foods, such as cheese, kimchi or sauerkraut, the flavour of miso becomes more complex the longer it is fermented. The smell is distinctive: when you walk into a miso store in Japan, you are greeted by a heady cloud of fragrance, reminiscent of freshly roasted coffee or melted dark chocolate.

The bible of Japanese food and culture, *Japanese Cooking: A Simple Art*, by Shizuo Tsuji, puts it like this: 'In many ways, miso is to Japanese cooking what butter is to French cooking and olive oil to the Italians.' I agree. It's just as central and just as ubiquitous and it does the same job too: it elevates everything it touches.

The first records of miso date from more than 2,500 years ago. It is believed that miso was brought to Japan by Buddhist priests from China during the seventh century. At the time, using fermented mixtures of salt, grains and soya beans was a common way of preserving food during the warmer months, and this practice formed the backbone to miso-making.

The original Chinese soya bean paste was transformed in Japanese cuisine into miso and shoyu (Japanese soy sauce), two hallmarks of the country's food. If you like Chinese food, you will have enjoyed fermented soya beans already in black bean, hoi sin or oyster sauces, in which they provide both the savoury umami flavour and the body, that all-enveloping mouthfeel.

There are hundreds of miso-producers in Japan and regional differences across the country, too. I like to compare the love for local miso in Japan to the pride in regional cuisine in Italy: there is

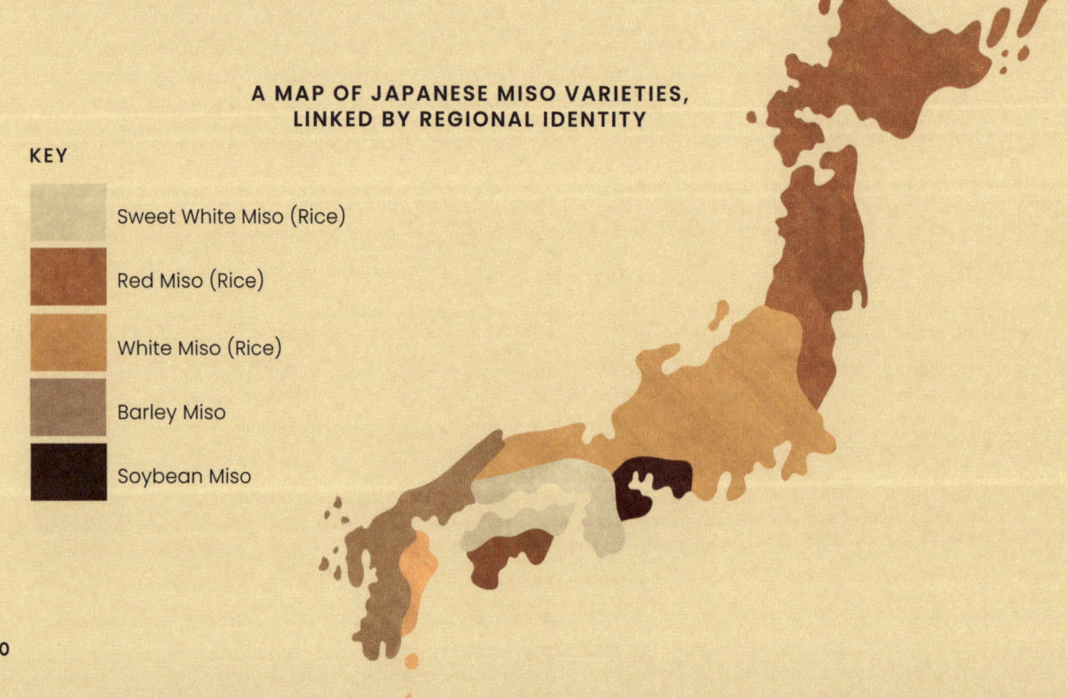

an insistence that their local miso is always the best in the country! In Japan, northern regions historically tended to make rice-based miso, as that is where most of the country's rice was farmed. The ancient capital of Kyoto is famous for its refined sweet rice miso, while southern parts of Japan prefer miso made from other grains, or simply pure soya bean miso.

In Japan, there is a lovely saying, *temae miso*, which translates roughly to 'blow your own trumpet', but literally means, 'I don't want to boast about my miso, but...' This is an unusual sentiment in Japanese culture, where humility is valued so highly. Clearly, in the case of homemade miso, all such modesty can be abandoned!

Historically, class defined what variety of miso you might eat. The upper classes or royalty would only eat rice miso made using expensive polished white rice. Rice miso was considered so special that it was given as a gift, or even used as currency. At the same time, peasants and farm hands were forbidden to use the rice they harvested to make their own miso, so many used broken rice, or other grains such as millet and barley, instead. This explains why miso made from these grains once had a reputation for being more rustic and less fancy. Today, though, miso made from different grains is considered special, as these are often made by artisans and in smaller batches.

In Japan, a bowl of miso soup has a huge nostalgic and cultural significance. It is a reminder of simpler times, the homemade breakfasts of childhood, comfort food, even a form of medicine. It is a hug in a bowl that has a timeless quality, similar to the famous healing powers of Jewish chicken soup. Though miso was once seen as a quintessentially Japanese ingredient, these days imaginative cooks have started to re-imagine its greater possibilities. Miso is now increasingly being enjoyed as a clever umami flavour booster and not just for adding a Japanese twist to your meal. For me, miso is the ancient cupboard staple I can't live without.

THE MANY TYPES OF MISO

Those new to miso are often surprised to learn that there are near-infinite varieties, just as there are countless different wines or cheeses.

If you adjust the ratio of soya bean to mould-inoculated grain to salt, or aspects of the environment, the length of fermentation, or the beans or grains chosen, you'll get a different type of miso. A wide range of flavours from mild to pungent, and textures from smooth to chunky, can result.

As you might imagine, I have a rather large collection of miso in my kitchen cupboards. In fact, it's a wonder that I have room for anything else! If you are thinking of starting to cook with miso regularly, red and white rice-based miso pastes are the most common in the recipes in this book, followed by sweet white miso, with *hatcho* (pure soya bean) and barley miso also making appearances. I would recommend starting with the more common red and white misos, which are used most widely in general cooking, then adding more specialist types as you become more familiar and expert.

There are so many different ways to categorize miso, so for simplicity's sake, I'll describe them here by the ingredients they contain and their length of fermentation.

RICE MISO (*KOME* MISO)

The most common type in Japan, making up more than 80 percent of the miso produced.
It is made from rice, soya beans and a bacterial culture. Salt is added and the mixture is left to ferment for (usually) 6 to 12 months.

Broadly speaking, a 6-month rice miso is called a *shiro* miso (white miso) and a 12-month or older

Sweet
white
saikyo
rice miso
Red
miso
White
miso
Pure
soybean
hatcho
miso
Barley
miso

rice miso is called *aka* miso (red miso). As for the use of the words 'white' and 'red' to describe them, these are literal translations and can be confusing, since the real-life colours do not match the descriptors perfectly. 'White' miso is actually the colour of wet sand, while 'red' miso comes in a range of browns, from terracotta to dark oak. This is the result of non-enzymic browning, a phenomenon whereby amino acids react with simple sugars to generate larger molecules which are browner in colour and deeper in taste.

A third type of rice miso – sweet white miso – is traditionally made in Kyoto, Japan's ancient capital and considered to be the most prestigious place to make refined miso. *Saikyo* miso, the most famous type, is the sweetest and lightest of the white misos. It is made with a large proportion of rice, a smaller proportion of soya beans and a weaker brine, giving a much more delicate flavour. I remember my first visit to a *saikyo* miso factory and tasting the local miso freshly harvested, still warm. It was like a custard-flavoured cookie dough. As it is fermented for such a short time, just as with soft cheeses, it's a lot less stable and is best kept in the refrigerator to maintain its delicate flavours. It is very soft and pliable.

In recent years, interest in miso as a health product has encouraged miso-makers to begin making brown rice miso (*genmai* miso). This has a deep, complex flavour, closer to barley miso and with more fibre than traditional white rice miso.

BARLEY MISO (*MUGI* MISO)

The rustic, less polished cousin of rice miso. Usually darker in colour and a bit chunky in texture, it is made from soya beans, barley koji mould and salt and is sometimes called 'country miso'. I am a big fan, because of its rounded, sweet, malty, winey flavours. Typically, those living in the southern parts of Japan – Honshu and the islands of Kyushu and Shikoku – prefer this type of miso.

You can tell a miso is made from barley by looking closely at it: you will see fine brown veins left from the grain. Those lines are known in Japanese as the barley's 'loin cloth', so barley miso is often referred to as 'loin cloth miso'! Some barley miso is aged for longer than rice miso; the mixture is higher in protein and lower in carbohydrates, so it is not as sweet and can take longer to ferment. Some younger barley miso has an almost pineapple fruitiness.

PURE SOYA BEAN MISO (*MAME* MISO)

This is a very different type of miso, as it contains no grain at all. It is made from soya beans, a koji mould and salt, and makes up less than 2 percent of the miso made in Japan today. The most famous type is *hatcho* miso, made in Nagoya in the Aichi prefecture, the only miso with a warrant to supply the Emperor of Japan.

Hatcho miso is easily identifiable as it is very dark, almost black in colour, with a consistency similar to fudge: it is slightly dry and crumbly, but can be cut cleanly with a knife. *Hatcho* miso has been taken on all Japanese expeditions to the South Pole, so it has a reputation for being able to survive in the toughest environments. For centuries, Japanese writers and gourmands alike have celebrated *hatcho* miso's savoury, chocolatey aroma and unique flavour. It has the highest protein but lowest salt, carbohydrates and water of any miso, making it the traditional choice of the samurai, who relied on food that was highly nutritious but easy to transport (it can be kept without refrigeration).

This miso requires a lengthy ageing process of two to three years. You can only call your product '*hatcho* miso' if it is made in the eighth district in Okazaki City (*hatcho* means 'eight'), in a similar way to how Champagne only earns the name if it is made in that specific region of France. I highly recommend a visit to the miso factories of the area (including Hayakawa and Ota, founded an astounding 600 years ago) to witness hundreds of handmade cedar barrels filled with fermenting miso; there are only a handful of these traditional miso-makers remaining in Japan and a visit to them is incredibly impressive and special.

THE FLAVOUR OF MISO

I remember the first time I visited a miso factory, more than 15 years ago. The extreme heat and scale of the operation was overwhelming. Every individual process of miso-making took up entire rooms the size of football pitches, often with stairwells and scaffolding to hold all the activities in place.

Back home, when I made my own miso, it was satisfying that I was able to replicate each step of the process within the confines of my kitchen work surfaces. That wasn't some special talent of mine: making miso is actually quite simple; much of the work is done by enzymes and heat over time and there are only a few ingredients. I'll show you how easy it is to make yourself at home on page 34.

Miso is traditionally made from the fermentation of whole cooked soya beans, usually with another cooked cereal grain such as rice or barley, which has been inoculated with a mould. The result is a thick paste with savoury and sweet notes.

Sometimes this is ground to a smooth paste by the manufacturer, or at home by the cook, to create a consistency that will melt easily into sauces or broths.

The reason why you can't see separate pieces of soya beans or rice in miso paste is due to the process of enzymic breakdown fermentation: all the enzyme groups capable of breaking down cellulose, starch, protein and hemicellulose should be present and active in order to make successful miso.

At the heart of miso-making is the mould called *Aspergillus oryzae*, a name that I have always struggled to pronounce with any accuracy. Most *Aspergillus* can produce aflatoxins, which are poisonous, but thankfully this type for miso-making is a non-toxin-producing mould. (We have the Chinese to thank for that, as they originally invented the process.)

The first step in making miso is to create koji: this is the 'starter'. If you are making a rice miso, then you will need to make a rice koji. If you are making a barley miso or a pure soya bean miso, then the mould is grown on those grains or beans instead. To make koji, the grain or bean is inoculated with the mould and becomes capable of starting the fermentation process by secreting breakdown enzymes.

Koji-making requires a continuous stirring process in a high-humidity environment, to encourage fungal mycelia to grow as its enzymes start to break down the grain. It takes 40–48 hours for the koji to be ready. (Don't worry, I don't expect you to make your own koji at home! It's easy to buy.)

Separately, soya beans are cleaned, cooked, then mixed with the koji in different ratios. Crudely speaking, the higher the ratio of rice, the sweeter the miso. The koji works on the grains and beans, turning the rice starches into sugar and breaking down the beans into amino acids.

After this, a ratio of 10 percent salt by weight is added to the blend, which halts nearly all microbiological activity by reducing the available water that could support the growth of any food pathogens. However, not everything is stopped: the enzymes present are not inhibited and continue to break down the mixture of soya beans and rice during the ageing process. It is this that leads to the transformation of the cooked beans and grains into magical miso.

For most of miso's history, it has been made in large ceramic vessels with lids, either at home, or on a larger scale in handmade cedar wood barrels. It is believed that the hundreds of kinds of bacteria living in the barrels themselves add their own character to the miso, just as they do in barrels for ageing whisky. A lid is put on the vessels, to reduce any contact with air during the fermentation process, then at least two tonnes of

MAKING TRADITIONAL MISO

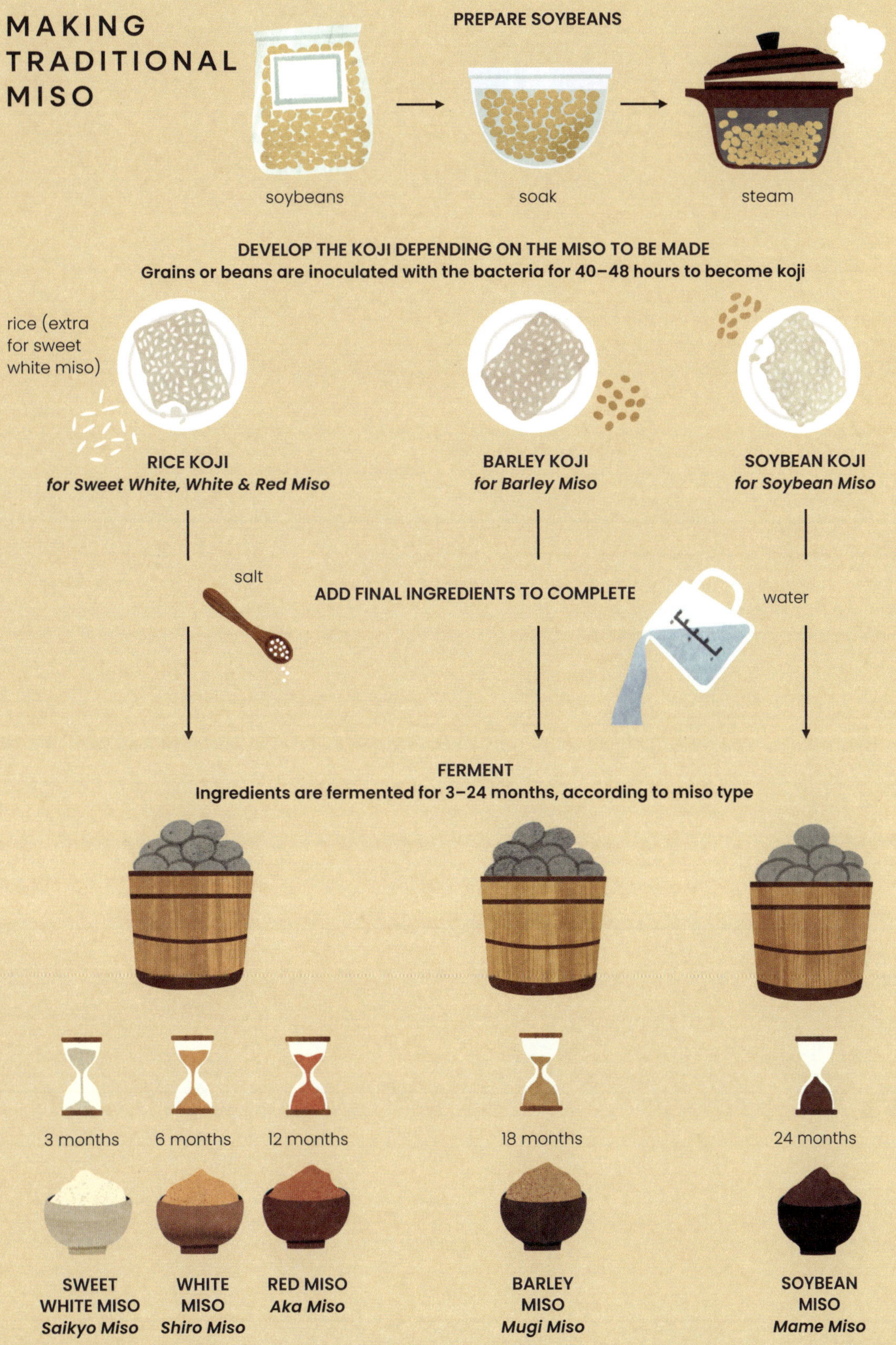

PREPARE SOYBEANS

DEVELOP THE KOJI DEPENDING ON THE MISO TO BE MADE
Grains or beans are inoculated with the bacteria for 40–48 hours to become koji

FERMENT
Ingredients are fermented for 3–24 months, according to miso type

3 months — **SWEET WHITE MISO** *Saikyo Miso*

6 months — **WHITE MISO** *Shiro Miso*

12 months — **RED MISO** *Aka Miso*

18 months — **BARLEY MISO** *Mugi Miso*

24 months — **SOYBEAN MISO** *Mame Miso*

rocks piled on top; arranged in such a way to prevent even an earthquake from toppling the barrels over, so precious is the paste inside. The ageing time for miso can be anything from three months to three years.

There are only a few manufacturers left who are making miso in this traditional way, in cedar barrels with no temperature controls, such as my friends at Noda Miso (see page 30) in the Aichi prefecture, and the two *hatcho* miso factories in the same region. Outside Japan, The American Miso Company (see page 30) has been replicating the traditional miso-making processes in North Carolina for almost 50 years: impressive!

Making miso is not an exact science, so each batch will vary slightly, but the main factors that impact on the fermentation and overall outcome will be the grain-to-bean ratio, the ageing time and the temperature. It is believed that the single most important factor in determining good umami flavour is fermentation and ageing time: the slower and more natural, the better.

OPPOSITE *Sano Miso* is a modern miso shop located in Kameido in Tokyo. You can taste over 60 types of miso from around Japan here, and purchase the miso by weight as well as have it packaged beautifully as a gift. Each miso type is displayed with cooking suggestions and its story of origin. This is truly a miso mecca with a delicious café inside serving miso dishes too.

500
吟醸仕込み
金亀子みそ 白こし
570円
京都
赤だしみそ 祇園

WHAT DOES MISO TASTE LIKE?

At the most simple level, miso is a savoury-tasting paste with notes of sweetness. It has a complexity that is hard to describe and, because there are so many different types, describing the characteristics of miso is like trying to describe 'wine' or 'cheese'; a generic description is unsatisfactory. To really appreciate the wonderful world of miso, I have tried to capture its wide spectrum of flavours overleaf.

This diagram (see page 20) attempts to showcase the range of types and colours of miso, with flavour notes. As you can see, miso can vary from sweet pudding flavours through to deep cocoa and coffee aromas. This complexity of flavour is very common in fermented ingredients, in which we can enjoy several flavour notes all at once, but all in balance.

If you are new to miso then you may not be aware of the incredible spectrum of flavours miso can bring. Overleaf are miso tasting notes for each type ranging from sweet tangy cheesy notes all the way through to smokey coffee flavours.

You will be hard-pressed not to find a miso to add deep yet complementary flavours to your dish.

In some restaurants in Japan, you can even pair different misos with red wines and cheese for some serious umami parties in your mouth.

UMAMI

It is impossible to talk about the flavours of miso without referring to umami. Throughout this book, I will talk about umami frequently, so it pays to understand what that really means.

Umami is the fifth taste, after sweet, salty, bitter and sour. It literally translates as 'pleasant savoury taste'. In my own non-technical language, I describe it as the deep and savoury 'oomph' you can sometimes detect in a dish. It is the difference between a light Camembert and an aged Parmesan, or a light onion gravy and a rich red wine gravy… the Parmesan and the rich gravy simply stimulate your tastebuds in a more profound way and, therefore, are deemed more flavourful.

On a scientific level, umami is the taste that is imparted by amino acids, predominantly glutamate and aspartate, as well as some ribonucleotides which are found in dashi (see page 40). The result is a meaty, savoury sensation in food. Umami was first discovered by Professor Kikunae Ikeda in 1908, but it was not until 2000 that it was taken seriously in the culinary world, when it was confirmed that specific sensors on the tongue are activated by glutamate, and umami was finally accepted as the fifth taste.

Miso scores high on umami; therefore adding it to dishes that are missing 'oomph' works a treat. It is particularly good with ingredients that already contain their own level of umami, such as cheese or tomato. In Japan, and in many Asian countries, umami is familiar as a concept: the pantry staples of soy sauce, fish sauce, rice vinegar and cooking wine all have high umami levels. In the west, while the word 'umami' has only taken hold in the last couple of decades, the principle is equally well established in cooking: cheeses, cured meats, ripe tomatoes, wine vinegars, Worcestershire sauce and mushrooms all have high levels of umami and are added to bring deeper flavours.

There is a belief that umami and its flavour sensations are part of an evolutionary purpose: sweetness in food indicates to the body the presence of carbohydrates for energy, and salt is needed for survival, while umami provides the stimulus for finding protein. Glutamate induces salivation, as well as satisfying hunger. Our bodies have been designed to seek out these umami sensations; most children love simple tomato and cheese pasta and that can be explained by their natural desire for umami. There is even much higher umami in human breast milk than in cow's milk. Umami is one of the most natural ways we have learned to satisfy our hunger and add flavour to our cooking.

Once you have got used to miso's superpowers in seasoning, it is hard to enjoy dishes without boosted levels of umami. You have been warned!

KOKUMI

This term is almost unheard of in the west. In Japanese, *koku* means 'body' and 'fullness' and *mi* means 'taste'. In most descriptions, it is said that kokumi's effects in the mouth are continuity, thickness and mouthfeel. It leads to a sensation of 'mouth-coating', in the same way as butter or molten chocolate embrace the entire palate.

Adding miso to certain dishes, especially broths, can create a noticeable kokumi effect. Kokumi can be considered an enhancer for the five basic tastes, as it magnifies and lengthens them. It was discovered in 1989, when calcium detectors on the tongue were shown to be activated by amino acids, specifically glutamate. While umami is triggered by single amino acids, kokumi is activated by (take a deep breath) amino acid groupings of glutamyl-derived di- and tri-peptides, such as the antioxidant glutathione. While kokumi is the subject of continuing research, it makes sense that amino acids that are a product of fermentation breakdown could be a good source. Other foods where it is found are fish sauce, yeast, soy sauce, cheeses and some beers.

While we can recognize the kokumi effect in miso recipes, it is not always obvious where umami stops and kokumi takes over (see page 189).

MISO FLAVOUR SPECTRUM

SWEET WHITE MISO (RICE MISO)

Custard, soya milk, butterscotch, Camembert cheese, cashew nuts

WHITE MISO (RICE MISO)

Buttery, cereal, toast, salted caramel, pine nuts, almonds, Cheddar cheese

RED MISO (RICE MISO)

Nutty, fruity, hearty, funky, parmesan

BARLEY MISO

Pineapple, fruity, earthy, pecorino cheese

BROWN RICE MISO

Light soy sauce, mushrooms, walnuts

PURE SOYA BEAN MISO

Smoky, coffee, dark/bittersweet chocolate, sweet soy sauce

MISO AND HEALTH

For hundreds of years, the Japanese have eaten miso as a health food. I remember a miso-maker telling me that, when he first heard of the Chernobyl nuclear disaster in 1986 and the Fukushima disaster in 2011, the first thing he did was send miso to the areas to support the victims. There is a strongly held belief in Japan that miso has an almost magical ability to cure and soothe the body, if eaten regularly; it's a sort of ancient superfood. Japanese adverts by soup companies market miso as something that always makes you feel better when you are unwell, hungover or even homesick!

When I was briefly in hospital in Japan, I was served miso soup throughout the day with fresh seasonal vegetables and fish. It is a balm for the soul and its role in healing is well-supported in Japanese culture.

The famously long lives of the Japanese have always been linked to their traditional diet, full of fermented ingredients such as shoyu (Japanese soy sauce) and miso. Certainly, Japanese food has a reputation for being healthy and, having travelled extensively around the country, I can report that this is largely true, especially in rural areas where most food is prepared from scratch and eaten at home. However, in big Japanese cities, fast food and busier lifestyles are taking their toll.

There is not a lot of research to back up the long-term impact of eating miso regularly, but there are a number of reasons why miso can support a healthy diet.

ANCIENT HEALTH REMEDY

Using soy in medicine dates back to the fourth century AD, when the celebrated Chinese doctor Ge Hong included miso in his book as a way to stop the common cold. This is the earliest record of miso being thought to have remedial properties. He even included a guide to matching the type of miso to the ailment: if you are feeling weak and cold, go for a dark and longer-fermented red miso or barley miso; if you are feverish, he recommended a lighter, sweeter miso.

FERMENTATION, UNPROCESSED FOODS AND GUT HEALTH

Miso can contain live good bacteria with probiotic properties, fantastic for the maintenance of a healthy gut, as these 'good bacteria' will replace the 'bad bacteria' colonizing the gut wall interface and thereby promote positive gut health.

In recent years, there has been research making a link between eating fermented foods regularly and both good gut health and better mental health. Professor Tim Spector, co-founder of ZOE, says that eating fermented foods is one of his top five tips for a healthier gut biome. He recommends eating a small amount of fermented foods every day and warns against the impact of eating processed foods, which are believed to contribute to poor microbiome health.

There is a general movement towards whole foods with natural simple ingredients that have undergone minimal processing. As miso is a product of fermentation and contains only beans, grains and salt, it is considered a super-clean food with natural flavour-boosting properties; a great swap for a processed stock cube.

To benefit from miso for your gut health, make sure you choose an unpasteurized miso and enjoy it in dressings, broths and sauces with no (or minimal) cooking. This will help to preserve more of its benefits.

DIGESTION

In Japan, miso soup is often served at the end of a multi-course meal to help with digestion, especially after more traditional set dinners such as *kaiseki*. Since the fermentation process breaks down 90 percent of miso's basic nutrients into simpler forms, it is very easy to digest. Miso soup is my go-to remedy to settle an uneasy stomach, or to soothe indigestion.

QUALITY PROTEIN

Most miso contains about 12 percent protein. Soy is a source of complete protein, containing all eight of the amino acids that our bodies need. Protein quality is measured by how much of the protein can be used by the body, expressed as NPU (net protein utilization). Eggs have an NPU score of 94, the highest of any known food. Chicken has 65 and miso has 72. While you are unlikely to be consuming that much miso by weight, this gives you a sense of how protein-rich miso is, and how eating it can provide more and better quality protein than many animal products.

LOW-FAT, LOW-CALORIE, HIGH SATIETY

Eating miso soup regularly can help to maintain a healthy weight: a typical miso soup contains fewer than 100 kcal and the protein keeps you feeling fuller for longer because it satiates. The science of satiety is complicated, but to keep it simple, of all the nutrients, it is protein that has the strongest effect on triggering satiety, and miso is a good source of protein. This is why, when I have a miso soup in the late morning, it takes the edge off my hunger so much that I can end up having a much later lunch.

ESSENTIAL VITAMINS

Miso contains vitamins E and B12, as well as many minerals. It is thought to be effective in reducing blood sugar and cholesterol, while some studies show that eating it regularly combats many signs of ageing too, by boosting the detoxing abilities of the body. Miso contains a source of essential vitamin B12, one of the vitamins most commonly deficient in the diets of vegetarians and vegans. It is also a natural source of vitamin K, an important nutrient in bone health.

HANGOVERS

Miso has a reputation for being a fantastic cure for hangovers. In fact, in vending machines across Japan, cans of miso soup are readily available next to bottles of hot green tea to bring you back to life after a heavy night. Choline, one of the B vitamins found in miso, helps to prevent the build-up of alcohol in the liver and speeds up its discharge from the body, so the next time you are regretting the night before, reach for a warming bowl of miso soup!

SALT

Many people are keen to reduce the amount of salt in their diets. The challenge is that salt is so good at bringing out flavours in food and there has not been a ready substitute for it. At first glance, miso has around 10 percent salt as part of its fermentation formula – which is of course high – but in the context of how much is used in each meal, the salt content from miso in a dish is no more (and often less) than in comparable miso-free meals. You will see that my recipes rarely call for the addition of salt, as all the saltiness in the dishes comes from miso itself.

As with all foods, I believe that the secret to healthy eating is in moderation. However, miso is a nourishing ingredient that not only tastes great, it makes us feel good when we are eating it too.

MISO AROUND THE WORLD

The future of miso is much, much brighter today than it was when I first wrote about it a decade ago.

Despite being the home of miso, in Japan, consumption has been in slow decline for the last 50 years. The growing popularity of western-style breakfasts and fast food has made it less relevant to the average young person with a busy lifestyle; waking up to the aromas of your mother's miso soup has become a distant memory. As a result, smaller miso factories are being snapped up by bigger players as demand falls, while the cost of the craft and the ingredients both remain high.

Meanwhile, the popularity of miso outside Japan has grown. This is to the great relief of miso-makers in Japan, who have pivoted their focus to exports to keep their businesses profitable. Not all miso-producers have benefited from this though, as only the biggest players can afford to compete on the international stage.

With this landscape in mind, it has been wonderful to witness, in the last few years, a mini-renaissance for miso within Japan. Since the Covid pandemic, more traditional meals with nostalgic overtones have been embraced once again in Japanese homes, with consumption of miso starting to show signs of recovery for the first time in five decades. Homemade miso classes are becoming commonplace in the country, as are businesses that celebrate miso; there are so many more miso-themed cafés, delis and restaurants now than there were when I first started visiting Japan 15 years ago.

Outside Japan, not only is miso being enjoyed as part of the wider adoption of Japanese food as a popular cuisine, but the use of miso as a flavour booster in non-Japanese food is also exploding. Cookery shows and cookbooks have been a big part of this change, with chefs and food writers around the world embracing the versatile umami powers of miso, regardless of which cuisine they specialize in. My work has been a small part of this re-imagination of miso and its role in the kitchen.

Pictured here (and overleaf) are some of my favourite miso shops in Japan. In these stores, miso is bought deli-style, by weight from barrels, alongside ready-made miso dips and pickles. Up to 60 types of regional miso are sold, as well as products to make miso soup, including bonito and kombu for dashi (see page 40), shiitake mushrooms and garnishes. There are miso-flavoured breads, cookies, crackers and sweets. Miso stores should be part of any visit to Japan; they demonstrate the importance of craft, history and expertise in Japanese food that is so central to the country's culture.

THE FUTURE OF MISO

When I first started my miso company, it was difficult to find anyone who even knew what miso was. I didn't appreciate at the time just how long it would take to educate my potential customers and establish the ancient eastern ingredient in the west. I was often a lone voice in pushing for miso to be used in other cuisines. But, in the last few years, that has started to change. I am delighted to now be part of a wider network of fermenters who are as obsessed with miso as I am and who are approaching miso-making from a macro, global perspective. In particular, the new wave of miso-makers want to see miso having a more sustainable role in our food ecosystem.

I want to introduce you to seven miso-makers who I believe represent the future of miso, each bringing something new to an ancient craft.

OPPOSITE *Mankyu Miso* is one of the oldest miso shops, located in Asakusa, Tokyo, selling a selection of specialist miso from around Japan. It has been in the family for many generations and is a must-see if you are visiting this area.

万久
万
お土産品
味自慢
あま酒
冷やし
アイスクリーム
江戸アイス
仙臺味噌
信州諏訪味噌
麦味噌
甘味噌
西京
白味噌
三州八丁味噌
しなの路
万久

DANIEL OECHSLER, MIEKO AZUMA and MELINA MUCKLE, founders of Miso Miso, GERMANY (misomiso.eu)

A charming little business set up by friends of Japanese and German origin in Heidelberg, Germany. They are miso obsessives who want the world to know that 'miso is not just for miso soup!' They make two types of rice miso, using locally grown chickpeas from Bavaria and soya beans from Baden-Württemberg. This local approach to sourcing is an important and recurring theme for the future of miso. Miso Miso even have a seasonal special which I am desperate to try: soya bean miso with dried apricots and walnuts for Christmas!

They say, 'For us, miso is the absolute secret ingredient for adding depth of flavour and exciting notes to our dishes. In fact, we use miso for everything; to refine a salad dressing, as a marinade for oven-baked vegetables with good olive oil, or as a replacement for salt in our morning porridge. We even make granola and chocolate brownies with miso – sweet variations are surprisingly good!'

DOUGLAS McMASTER, chef and founder of Silo, the world's first zero-waste restaurant, and founder of Fermentation Factory, the UK's first dedicated koji-making facility (douglasmcmaster.com)

I have long been an admirer of Doug. A legendary chef and visionary leader in the future of food, he uses his deep knowledge of ingredients, flavour and fermentation to create successful businesses that balance commercial success with pioneering sustainability. His restaurant-with-no-bin, where nothing goes to waste, sparked his journey into miso.

For Doug, koji is a game-changing ingredient. While traditional miso is made from koji plus a premium product such as soya beans or chickpeas, Doug applies koji's qualities to food waste, a matter close to his heart and which has become a global issue for the food industry. His restaurant Silo ferments all food scraps into various garums and misos, which are then returned to the menu at a later date.

I have been lucky to try a whole range of ferments created by Doug and his team, including miso made from lemon husks, seed pulp, mushroom trimmings and cheese rinds. A sweet and buttery bread miso remains my favourite. These ingredients would have ended up in the bin, or composted, had they not been fermented with fava beans, their chosen substrate for their miso, which is both sustainable and affordable. As Doug observes, 'Miso is pigeonholed into Japanese cuisine, but my restaurant is not British or Japanese, yet there is miso all over it'.

When Doug and his team travelled to Japan to share their creations, they had been prepared to be dismissed, but quite the contrary, they were met with, 'Glee, fascination, and massive amounts of encouragement.' Doug's passion for miso moves me: 'I want miso to be in every refrigerator in the country in the future. It is an extraordinary product. It has an inner potential to be entirely sustainable. It will sit in your refrigerator for a really long time, it will immediately give every dish a kind of magic wand of flavour. Bland dishes become delicious dishes, it is healthy… it is gastronomically elite! Why would you starve yourself of umami? I want to see a domino effect around the world. Add miso to Mexican food, French food, any food – miso will just make everything better.' Doug eats miso every day and recommends always reaching for miso when making gravy.

His latest project, the Fermentation Factory, aims to offer restaurants and home cooks the opportunity to purchase fresh koji and ferment their own food waste into miso. His vision is exemplary and I can only imagine the scale of his contribution in years to come, if making your own miso from food waste becomes commonplace.

OPPOSITE *Misogen* is a miso café in Tokyo station, serving a variety of miso soups throughout the day, made from artisan miso from around Japan.

KENJI MORIMOTO, Digital Creator and Author of Ferments, UK (@kenjcooks)

Kenji is a Japanese American whose relationship with miso is deeply entwined with his family history and identity. He has memories of enjoying miso throughout his childhood and calls it 'the flavour of home'. Kenji found miso-making to be a source of peace and comfort during the Covid pandemic. 'I was surprised how making miso during lockdown really connected me more deeply with my Buddhism, where the emphasis of patience and trust, and being mindful in the fermentation process, taught me to slow down and be more present. Miso-making brought me catharsis and peace.'

His favourite ferments include chickpea and pumpkin miso and his inspiration is driven by a mix of curiosity and the desire to use up ingredients that are in abundance, or nearing expiration. He believes that fermentation is a great tool for reducing food waste, whether that is mandarin peel or even an unloved chocolate cake. He also loves to use miso as a pickling bed in his ferments, which is a traditional Japanese way to preserve vegetables, called misozuke (see page 89 for my recipe).

Kenji believes that miso can transcend cultural boundaries, both because it is so versatile and because it satisfies the universal craving for umami and salty flavours. He is unashamedly relaxed about the definition of what miso can be and believes miso-making should be inclusive and creative. As long as traditional methods are followed, he thinks all variations can still be considered miso. He loves to use his miso in non-Japanese dishes.

This is *Misotetsukagiroi*, a miso izakaya in Tokyo. All their dishes celebrate miso from around Japan, and it is one of the pioneering restaurants of its kind. Sit amongst Japanese antiques and enjoy this modern take on miso.

PRACHET SANCHETI, Brown Koji Boy, INDIA (brownkojiboy.com)

Prachet's unique approach to miso-making is influenced by the tropical climate and flavours of Goa, where he is based. He uses local ingredients – chana dal, millet and even a Goan bread – to make his miso. 'We're playing with flavours that highlight local crops while still preserving the deep umami richness that defines miso. It's a balance – innovating without losing the essence.'

He believes that miso can add a lot of depth to Indian cuisine. He adds it to dal and curries; he blends it with butter and sautés it with vegetables, then enjoys it with upma*, a popular Indian breakfast dish. He also recommends lacing* khichdi *with his spiced chickpea miso, or using cashew miso in creamy curries such as paneer makhani and korma. 'Adding miso to coconut and tamarind chutneys also intensifies their savouriness, while keeping the core flavours intact.'*

JONATHAN HOPE, founder of Kultured (kultured.co.uk)

I met first Jonathan when he came to see me in my office and presented me with a 'Happy Meal miso' and a 'Haribo miso'. I was intrigued, to say the least! Jonathan pushes the boundaries of what is and what is not miso, with a nod to not taking it too seriously. He believes that fermentation, at its heart, is experimental and should be inclusive.

Outside of his playful miso experiments, Jonathan makes a line of miso for chefs, made from sustainable UK-grown grains rather than from traditional soya beans. This intrigued me, since even Japanese miso-manufacturers rarely buy soya beans from Japan due to their steep cost. His range includes pink flamingo miso, fava bean miso, badger bean miso and marrowfat pea miso, which – apart from having fabulous names – are each delicious and distinctive in their own way.

Jonathan's approach is not only novel and sustainable but also commercially savvy. 'It did not make sense for me to make traditional miso with soya beans, to then compete with traditional Japanese miso. By working with UK beans, I found myself a nice differentiation in the market which was also sustainable – it is an approach that felt authentic to me.'

Like me, Jonathan gets frustrated that not everyone knows how to cook with miso, when he uses it every day. 'I love it neat on bread, on potatoes, in lasagne, in everything really! Miso should be a common ingredient, not reserved for Japanese dishes.' Jonathan predicts that miso will become just as common as salt and pepper in the future, and that restaurants will use miso to enhance flavours without needing to call it out on the menu. His career highlight so far has been impressing Jamie Oliver with his 'Greggs Sausage Roll miso'.

KIYOE NODA, Noda Miso, JAPAN (masuzuka.co.jp)

The family behind Noda Miso are wonderful, and I'm proud to say they are friends of mine. We stayed at their factory in the Aichi prefecture many years ago, to capture on film their whole miso-making process. Here, they have been making miso in the same way since 1928, following the traditional 18-month process of pure natural fermentation, with no temperature controls, only the climate. They age their miso in more than 400 traditional Japanese cedar or hinoki cypress wooden barrels, or rather what is left of them, since the makers of these barrels are no longer in business and the barrels eventually collapse with use. There is even a room in the factory that is lined completely with the collapsed panels of miso barrels: it is quite a moving experience to be enveloped in this warm room, faintly scented, still, with the miso the barrels used to hold so tightly.

I have included this lovely business because I believe there is a place in the future for traditional miso-makers to keep doing what they have always done. These tend to be family businesses, so the challenge is all in the handing on of the baton to their children. I hope to see the survival and growth of miso-makers such as Noda Miso, who work so hard to keep their legacy and business alive in the face of mass miso production in Japan.

Noda Miso is probably the most beautiful and serene factory I have ever visited. The rooms where the miso is aged are dark and quiet, apart from the gentle classical music that is played to the miso to nurture its growth. They also have a programme of bringing in local schoolchildren to learn all about miso-making, in an attempt to engage their community. Long live these businesses: support small artisanal producers when you can.

CODY SMITH, 'Miso master', The American Miso Company, USA (@misomaster)

In the foothills of Rutherfordton, North Carolina, you will find the most incredible miso factory, founded 45 years ago and replicating the miso-making methods of ancient Japan. Despite its name, The American Miso Company make all the traditional styles – sweet white, red, barley and brown rice miso – without adaptations. Cody uses only natural fermentation processes, with no heat treatment or yeast to speed up the umami flavour development. Every step of the process is handmade, using only organic ingredients. In fact, I would go as far as saying that their approach is more 'traditional' than many of the miso-manufacturers I have visited in Japan!

North Carolina might seem like an unusual location to make miso, but it was selected specifically because of its distance from cities and pollution, while its climate includes four equal-length seasons, giving the best fermentation environment. I am impressed with just how closely this factory replicates authentic miso-making. 'We religiously stick to those historical ways in which miso has been made for centuries,' says Cody. This gives me hope that the traditional ways of making miso will not die off in Japan, since other countries can learn to adopt the same practices too.

When showcasing miso at trade shows, the company focuses on how versatile it is, demonstrating miso pesto, miso peanut Thai curry sauces, miso barbecue sauces, even miso maple syrup, which has a salted caramel flavour.

Cody Smith comes from a line of family members who have worked at The American Miso Company and is proud to take on the baton of tradition. 'I would hope that, in 20 years, miso becomes a staple in everybody's refrigerator, because they have finally understood the powers of miso.'

CAN ANYTHING BE MISO'D?

With so many new approaches to miso-making, where the traditional ingredients are swapped for alternatives, you might ask if there is anything that can't be miso'd.

Miso is part of a family called amino pastes. Amino acids are the result of proteins that have been broken down and this is where the umami taste originates. We think that the process began in China, with the making of another soya bean paste called *jang*. Many Asian countries have their own ways of making amino pastes, such as gochujang in Korea, each with their own distinctive qualities. You can make a miso from any material that contains a high level of protein: seeds, beans and nuts are ideal as they have a protein source to support germination, plus a good source of carbohydrate or fat to provide energy. A high-protein ingredient (such as soya beans), a carbohydrate fermentation culture (such as cereal koji), salt and time are the essential ingredients of miso.

If you are experimenting with miso-making in less traditional ways, watch out for ingredients with a high fat content, as they run the risk of generating too much oil, leading to a rancid taste. Some oils are higher in unsaturated fats, which can turn sour more quickly than saturated fats.

COOKING WITH MISO: RULES AND TIPS

After decades as my go-to seasoning, adding miso to my cooking has become a reflex for me, an automatic step when I'm finishing a dish. But, of course, it was not always like that: we only get good at something with lots of practice, and that means getting it wrong sometimes.

With all my experience, I can now share with you the most important lessons in how to use miso to magical effect. I have come to know some common mistakes that can ruin a perfectly good dish and I want you to avoid them!

The first thing you should know is that there is no need to be at all intimidated, as the Japanese pantry is designed for the home cook's success. In one of my favourite books on Japanese food, *Sushi and Beyond*, author Michael Booth compares French and Japanese cuisines. He explains that, while the French prepare everything from scratch, processes are long and you need a high level of skill to get it right at home, Japanese food is almost the opposite, 'all of it prepared with the minimum of meddling from the chef and a deep respect for the ingredients.'

Each item in the Japanese pantry, whether it be soy sauce, miso, rice vinegar or mirin, has already been through a carefully crafted process, aged for years to reach the optimum flavours before being packaged up for the home cook. The technical preparation has been left to the experts, while the home cook has the delightful task of simply making the most of the finished product. By the time a jar of miso enters your shopping bag, the hard work has already been done.

By taking my advice, miso will quickly become your secret weapon, making all your meals mightier. It is perfect for the busy person who wants deep tasty flavours but does not have time to mess around with reductions and long, complicated processes.

Here are my key rules for cooking with miso:

1) AVOID BOILING

The complex flavours of miso – as well as some of its nutritional benefits – are damaged when it is heated at prolonged high temperatures. This is why miso is traditionally stirred in at the final stages of cooking, either at a gentle simmer or with the heat turned off. If miso is added at the start of making a dish, it can lose its subtle balance of sweet and savoury tones.

2) STRAIN MISO FOR SOUPS AND BROTHS

Miso is thick and sticky, like peanut butter or set honey. But, unlike those ingredients, it does not react well to heat: instead of becoming more pliable when warmed up, it becomes harder and drier. If you try to stir miso directly into a large volume of liquid, you will be faced with lumpy broth or sauce.

In all my soup and sauce recipes, therefore, I advise that you strain the miso into the broth. The Japanese – who have a gadget for everything – have come up with a clever tool for this. The miso paste is put inside a miso strainer and immersed into the broth with one hand, while the other hand stirs the paste into the liquid from inside the strainer, allowing the miso to slowly 'melt' into the broth with no risk of lumps. You can use a small sieve (strainer), tea strainer or a ladle to mimic the same process, or you can simply place the miso paste in a separate small bowl, then ladle in liquid from the main pot, before whisking the miso mixture until smooth. Finally, pour everything in the bowl back into the main pot, where the miso will melt effortlessly in.

3) THIN MISO FOR SAUCES

To avoid lumps of miso in dressings and sauces, always thin it out first. Unlike with a lot of salad dressings – where you can throw all your ingredients into a bottle and shake – miso would remain lumpy, clinging on to your salad leaves in an unappetizing way. I recommend that you thin the miso with a similar volume of another liquid – perhaps olive oil or water – mixing them in a bowl with a spoon or small whisk until completely smooth. This step produces a thick liquid that can be readily folded into the rest of the ingredients without lumps.

4) LOOK FOR UNPASTEURIZED MISO FOR HEALTH BENEFITS

For better flavour and for the full health benefits, choose unpasteurized miso where possible, so you know it has not undergone prolonged heat treatment. Unpasteurized miso in Japan is packed in boxes with a one-way valve, to allow the gas that is part of fermentation to be released, so that's one way to spot it.

5) TOOMAMI: a little goes a long way!

'Toomami' is the word I use when I see a dish with too many sources of umami, or a recipe which contains so much miso that it has become unbalanced. When seasoning a dish with miso, or making a sauce, beware of adding too much. When making a broth, add a little at a time: miso soup should be refreshing and savoury rather than salty.

When marinating with miso, blot fish or meat that has been coated with miso with some kitchen paper (paper towel) before cooking. The salt content of miso can dry out your protein if you put too much on. Consider each mouthful in balance: if you are making miso aubergines (eggplants) and the aubergines are quite small, don't lather a thick layer of miso on top; keep it subtle, you want to taste as much aubergine as miso. If you are making a sauce, beware of adding more than two sources of umami. When making desserts, you want to be able to taste the fruit, chocolate or whatever, so keep the miso light and add just a teaspoon at a time.

6) HOW TO STORE MISO

Miso should always be stored in a covered container. To maintain its colour and flavour, it is best to refrigerate it. As a general rule, the lighter the colour of the miso, the more careful you will need to be. Some miso is sold in plastic pouches, and I highly recommend decanting those into a resealable jar in your refrigerator and marking it with the date on which you opened the packet.

Sweet white miso should be consumed within three weeks of opening and white miso ideally within three months. Darker misos – such as barley, brown rice and red miso – keep at their best for at least six months and soya bean miso for 12 months. Beyond these periods, the miso will not spoil, but the flavour, texture and colour will change a lot and they will become less aromatic and complex in flavour. Soya bean miso, which contains much less salt, becomes harder, too.

If you see your miso forming white or green mould on top, simply skim it off, as you might with jam. Pinkish moulds are a more serious matter; you will need to scrape very deeply and use the remaining untainted miso within the next day or two, or throw it out. (I have met many miso-makers who claim that a lot of the umami is in the mould, so they happily whip it back into the miso! I don't do this, but applaud the brave souls who do...)

Batch by batch, there are natural variances to miso, but another of its quirks is a sensitivity to light. Miso changes colour from light to dark with time and temperature. White miso ultimately turns into red miso over time. To tackle this, I recommend that you keep your miso in a dark cupboard until you open it. Once opened, keep it in the refrigerator. If you get through miso at the rate that I do (a jar a week!) then you can just keep it in the cupboard with your other seasonings.

HOMEMADE MISO

Making miso at home will not recreate exactly the same results as you would find in the shops, but you might prefer it! First of all, it will be much less smooth and will have a more crumbly, dry texture that you might choose to smooth out using a mortar and pestle. Secondly, the flavours will vary. Remember that part of the variance in miso-making is determined by where you make it and the natural bacteria in the environment, as well as by the raw materials you choose. Just as whisky can be aged in a particular way to develop a desired flavour, so too can you create unique miso flavours from your own home.

A basic rice miso is both very achievable and a fun project. I have taught miso-making many times and the results are reliable, whether you have come to an in-person class in London or dialled in online from Boston.

Follow these steps carefully and, after six to nine months, you will enjoy a tasty, super-satisfying homemade miso. The process itself is actually incredibly easy, it's the waiting around for it to mature that's hard!

With fermentation, temperature is key. If you start your miso in the autumn, it will need more than six months before it can be eaten. During the summer, fermentation will be faster due to the warmer ambient temperatures, but the chances of moulds growing will also be higher. Late November to early March is thought the best time to make miso and, for some Japanese families, it is an annual tradition that everyone performs together. When choosing the vessel to make your miso, glass jars are good, as they allow you to see what's happening inside. A ceramic pot also works well and is traditional. Just make sure you have a secure way of closing the vessel and that it is filled to at least 80 percent capacity.

In the recipe here, miso is made by combining cooked soya beans with a rice koji mould, which acts as a fermentation starter. (Koji can be bought from specialist online stores.) When choosing your koji, there are two types: a firm granular koji and those sold in sheets. The latter type is easier to buy outside Japan, because it does not require refrigeration, but the granular type is considered more effective in breaking down proteins and carbohydrates in the miso, so it's worth it, if you can get hold of it! This recipe will work with both types.

Apart from salt to prevent the growth of further mould, there are no other ingredients apart from your patience...

MAKES ABOUT 4 KG/9 LB

1.3 kg/3 lb dried organic soya beans
1.8 kg/4 lb rice koji
500 g/1 lb 2 oz fine sea salt

TIP: When the miso is ready, you can blend it in a food processor or mortar and pestle for a smoother finish, or keep it rustic by enjoying it just the way it is! The miso can continue fermenting for up to 3 years, with the flavours becoming more and more complex and the paste becoming darker in colour and drier in texture.

Soak the soya beans in water overnight, then rinse and drain.

Tip the beans into a large saucepan or a pressure cooker. Cover with fresh water, bring slowly to the boil, then simmer for 4 hours in a saucepan or 45 minutes in a pressure cooker until the beans are soft and break easily when pressed between your fingers. Strain the beans over a large bowl, reserving the cooking liquid.

If using rice koji sheets, in a separate bowl, break the sheets into granules until all the pieces are separated. Mix in 50 g/1¾ oz salt until all is combined well. If using loose rice koji granules, simply mix with the 50 g/1¾ oz salt.

In a jug, measure 500 ml/18 fl oz of the cooking liquid from the soya beans and stir in 70 g/2½ oz more salt.

Continues overleaf

Tip the cooked soya beans into a large tray at least 7.5 cm/3 in deep. Crush them with a metal potato masher until they begin to break down; they will start to form a paste after about 20 minutes of mashing.

Next, add the koji and salt mix, then pour in the measured liquid gradually, while mixing all the ingredients with your hands. A dough-like paste will start to form; you will know it contains enough liquid when you throw a ball of it against a hard surface and it doesn't crumble. If it does, it is too dry; if it splatters, you have added too much liquid.

Form the paste into pieces the size of golf balls, pressing together firmly so that the balls are tightly packed.

Choose the container(s) for your miso to ferment in and clean it punctiliously with clear alcohol, such as vodka. A ceramic container with a tightly fitting lid is ideal, or sterilized glass jars with lids. If you are using a large pot, throw the miso balls into it with some force, to knock out any air in the balls. If you are filling jam jar-sized vessels, you will need to press the balls in, making sure that there are no air pockets in the jar. Once the vessel is full, flatten the surface and sprinkle the remaining salt across the top. The salt prevents mould from growing, so make sure there is plenty on top and around the edges. Cover with clingfilm (plastic wrap) and secure the lid. Find a heavy weight to place on the lid, to further reduce the chance of any air entering the vessel.

Store in a cool, dark cupboard. After 3 months, it is worth opening the container to check for any mould growth; there shouldn't be any, but, if you find some, simply scrape it off with a clean spoon. The miso should transform after 6 months, changing to a darker colour and a smoother consistency, as the fermentation continues.

SA-SHI-SU-SE-SO

This little-known formula underpins practically all Japanese food.

When I first learned about Sa-Shi-Su-Se-So, I was amazed how little it was known, as it's quite simply brilliant. It is one of those formulas that, once you have understood it, you will never forget when cooking.

For me, Sa-Shi-Su-Se-So is the A-B-C of Japanese cooking: the building blocks, literally the alphabet of seasoning excellence. The five characters are the consecutive letters of the third line of the Japanese Hiragana phonetic lettering system, taught to all learners of the language.

This widely known expression is passed down from parent to child to teach them how to flavour food properly, containing the secrets of an orderly precision to layering flavour. It neatly summarizes the five essential elements in Japanese seasoning, containing as it does the words from one of the characters of each ingredient in Japanese.

Sa さ (sugar: SA-to)

Shi し (salt: SHI-o)

Su す (vinegar: SU)

Se せ (soy sauce: SE-uyu, the traditional word for shoyu)

So そ (mi-SO)

Once you have learned the key principles, they can guide you each time you are seasoning dishes. For me, the structure and flavour journey that the rules deliver helps to explain why some dishes are just so universally popular. Think sweet-and-sour pork, teriyaki salmon, ketchup, pickles and barbecue sauces. Each follows this journey of sweetness hit first, then saltiness, then acidity and finally an umami note.

The Sa-Shi-Su-Se-So rule has truly shaped the way I have designed my recipes in this book. I hope it will become a memorable mantra for you too.

SA さ

(sugar: SA-to)

SHI し

(salt: SHI-o)

SU す

(vinegar: SU)

SE せ

(soy sauce: SE-uyu, the traditional word for shoyu)

SO そ

(mi-SO)

DASHI

Dashi is the stock base for a few dishes in this book. It is one of the key cornerstones of Japanese cuisine, just as chicken stock is for European food.

Its role in cooking is slightly different to that of European stock and takes a little explaining. On its own, dashi tastes unremarkable and you might wonder why there is so much fuss about it. The reason for the blandness is that glutamate – a measure of umami – on its own does not (counter-intuitively) taste of umami. In isolation, glutamate has been described as salty, sometimes soapy. But, for me, that is part of what makes this understated ingredient even more special: it is silently powerful.

Unlike chicken or fish stock, where you can pick out the flavours, dashi is so subtle that it can be overlooked even when you are searching for it. Its superpower lies in boosting all the flavours in a dish, making them taste like the best version of themselves. The glutamates in dashi are active at very low concentrations (as little as 0.01–0.03 percent by weight) which is ten times lower than those of table salt. It has an interactive effect on the other tastes and its impact lasts longer than that of salt, leading to a sense of deliciousness, fullness and roundness.

In my cooking classes, I like to illustrate this by submerging plain fried aubergine (eggplant) chunks in dashi. Within a few minutes, the aubergine tastes sweeter and creamier and all the bitter notes have disappeared, while the dashi has added a long savoury quality that lingers in your mouth. It is absolutely remarkable once you have tried it. Umami intensifies sweetness, moderates sourness and masks bitterness. Dashi perfects foods, so when you add it to sauces and broths, all the flavours are boosted and more rounded.

What is the secret behind this magic? Umami of course! We already know that this fifth taste was discovered by Professor Ikeda, but he did not stop there. He decided to identify the greatest umami combo possible, using Japanese ingredients.

The winning combination that he settled on is dashi. It is made from kombu (dried Japanese kelp), bonito flakes (aged skipjack tuna, anchovies or sardines dried and shaved into flakes) and aged shiitake mushrooms. Dashi is bountifully rich in naturally occurring glutamates and bursting with literally the most intense umami flavour possible. In fact, the most famous flavour enhancer in the world – MSG – was based on dashi... and was formulated by Professor Ikeda as well!

To make your dashi vegetarian-friendly, the bonito can be removed, so it is just kombu and shiitake mushrooms that deliver the umami. I personally love using vegetarian dashi in most of my cooking, as the smoky flavours of bonito can be a little overwhelming in some dishes.

DASHI AND MISO SOUP

To make traditional miso soup (see page 44), a blend of miso pastes are stirred into dashi, which supercharges the already umami-rich miso to booming levels of deep, lingering flavours. The soup tastes sweeter and has more umami: your whole mouth is coated in a rich savoury flavour. Dashi makes the difference between listening to a solo artist and a full orchestra. If you have always made miso soup using just hot water, try it with dashi and you will soon realize why this is the proper way.

How does it work? Food science is full of surprises and this is certainly one of them. Essentially, the glutamates in the miso and kombu interact with the five ribonucleotides found in the bonito, kombu and shiitake mushrooms. These materials can deliver umami separately, but together they deliver a mind-blowing 1 + 1 = 5, where the levels of umami detected have multiplied. In other words, the umami in dashi is more than the sum of its parts.

MAKING DASHI

MAKES 1 LITRE/1¾ PINTS

20 g/¾ oz piece of kombu (about two 20 x 5 cm/ 8 x 2 in strips)
1 litre/1¾ pints water
6 aged shiitake mushrooms
25 g/1 oz dried bonito flakes/ katsuobushi (optional)

TIP: If you are time-pressed, you can opt for instant dashi powder or a dashi teabag, to which you simply add hot water. If you are avoiding additives, look carefully at the ingredients, as these shortcuts often contain artificial flavourings and added sugar and salt to mimic the natural flavours of dashi.

While dashi might seem a little mysterious on a scientific level, making it is very straightforward – far easier than making, say, the French equivalent: a consommé.

With dashi, the hard work has already been done for you. Each of the ingredients in dashi has been aged to perfection, the kombu dried for at least a year and both the shiitake mushrooms and bonito aged (usually) for a minimum of two years. All we have to do at home is soak, simmer and strain.

For a vegetarian or lighter dashi, follow the first part of the recipe only and skip the bonito flakes.

Brush the kombu gently of any dust, but do not wash it; the white coating is where a lot of the flavour is. Using kitchen scissors, cut a couple of slits into the kombu to increase its surface area and soak it in a saucepan in the measured water along with the shiitake mushrooms for 1–2 hours.

Set the saucepan over a medium heat and slowly bring the kombu and shiitake mushrooms to the boil. Once you see bubbles at the edges of the pan, remove the kombu and mushrooms and turn off the heat. (If you leave the kombu in too long, it can make the dashi slimy and bitter-tasting.)

If you are making a vegetarian dashi, or prefer lighter-tasting dashi, then it is now complete.

To make a traditional dashi, add the bonito flakes and return the liquid to the boil, skimming off any impurities. Reduce the heat and simmer for another 30 seconds, then turn off the heat and allow the bonito flakes to sink to the bottom of the pan.

After 10 minutes, strain the dashi into a bowl through a sieve (strainer) lined with kitchen paper (paper towels). Gently squeeze the kitchen paper over the bowl to release any remaining dashi.

If you are not using the dashi straight away, store in a sealed container or clean bottle and keep in the refrigerator for up to 5 days. You can also portion it up and store it in the freezer for up to 3 months.

If you love Japanese food, this chapter is for you; I've stuffed it full of all the miso 'hall of fame' dishes your heart could desire.

Miso has played a key role in the Japanese pantry for centuries, relied upon as a quick route to deeply savoury umami flavours. It also has the power, when combined with other Japanese store cupboard items, to speedily form the basis of a vast array of Japanese dishes.

Miso + dashi = miso soup
Miso + mirin = marinade
Miso + rice vinegar = tasty miso dressing

So it's no surprise that miso is as ubiquitous and essential in Japan as salt and pepper is in the west.

In the pages that follow, I will help you master the classics, such as miso soup, ramen, miso cod and miso aubergines (eggplants), with recipes I have perfected for years, so you can replicate your favourites easily at home. Miso shines through as a lead flavour in these dishes, enhanced with dashi in broths, or balanced against sweetness and acidity in sauces and marinades.

You'll find I have included plenty of tips and tricks to ensure you learn the techniques of how to cook with miso just as much as the recipes themselves, because that is the key to success. I want you to be able, eventually, to recreate these timeless dishes effortlessly and expertly, using the knowledge you have gleaned from these pages.

Give these recipes a go, whether you are hosting guests or just wanting to make something a little bit special for you and your household.

THE QUINTESSENTIAL JAPANESE INGREDIENT

MISO SOUPS

A miso cookbook must start with a classic miso soup. No doubt your first encounter with miso was in such a soup, served at a Japanese restaurant. It is a classic for a reason, so you will find here my formula for how to make the timeless favourite, plus four further variations on the theme, just to keep life interesting.

1. DASHI BASE

You will need:

200 ml/7 fl oz dashi per portion, made from kombu, shiitake mushrooms and bonito flakes (optional). See page 40 for my Dashi recipe. Or you can use an instant powdered dashi, but check it doesn't contain artificial flavourings or added sugar or salt.

2. BLEND OF MISO PASTES

You will need:

½ tbsp light miso paste and ½ tbsp dark miso paste per portion. White and red miso pastes make a great starting point. You can also play with the ratios: the more light miso you include in the blend, the sweeter the broth will taste.

3. TOPPINGS

You will need:

1–2 tbsp toppings per portion

Choose ingredients that are small in size and gentle in flavour, such as chopped spring onions (scallions), sweetcorn, chopped fresh chives or parsley leaves, spinach, chopped carrots or chopped tofu.

MISOSHIRU

CLASSIC MISO SOUP WITH WAKAME AND TOFU

SERVES 4 AS A SNACK, STARTER (APPETIZER) OR SIDE DISH

---

2 tbsp dried wakame seaweed
1 litre/1¾ pints Dashi (see page 40)
200 g/7 oz firm tofu, cut into 1 cm/½ in cubes
2 tbsp white miso
3 tbsp red miso
2 spring onions (scallions), finely sliced

TIP: To preserve the flavours and nutrients of miso, it is best not to boil it. Always add it at the end of the dish, either when ingredients are at a low simmer, or with the heat turned off.

The mark of a good miso soup is in its contrasting colours and textures: pristine white tofu cubes floating on the surface of a cloudy broth, lined with crunchy curls of seaweed and sprinkled with aromatic spring onions (scallions). The clean, light flavours of the toppings ensure that the unique sweet and savoury flavours of the miso remain centre-stage in this ancient superfood.

Put the wakame in a small bowl, cover fully with cold water and set aside for 5 minutes until it has fully expanded.

Make the dashi and heat in a saucepan until it reaches a rolling boil. Add the tofu to the dashi and cook for 1 minute, before adding the rehydrated, drained seaweed.

The last stage is to add the miso paste, but it is important that the miso is not boiled. Reduce the heat so the dashi is at a simmer. Place both types of miso in a ladle or sieve (strainer). Dip the ladle or sieve into the saucepan so the dashi seeps in, but the miso does not escape into the pot. Turn off the heat. Slowly loosen up the miso with a spoon inside the ladle or sieve as the dashi mixes with it; the paste will slowly melt into the dashi.

Once all the miso has dissolved into the broth, scatter with the spring onions to add colour and fragrance.

TONJIRU

SLOW-COOKED PORK AND VEGETABLE MISO SOUP

SERVES 4

- 1 rack of baby back ribs
- 2 garlic cloves, finely chopped
- 1 tsp peeled and finely grated root ginger
- 1 litre/1¾ pints Dashi (see page 40), or vegetable stock
- 1 large carrot, peeled and chopped into 1.5 cm/5/8 in cubes
- 100 g/3½ oz daikon, peeled and chopped into 1.5 cm/5/8 in cubes
- 50 g/1¾ oz red miso
- 1½ tbsp white miso
- 1 spring onion (scallion), finely chopped

This was one of the first Japanese dishes I learned to cook and it's a comforting, rib-sticking soup. While it takes some time on the stove, it doesn't require much supervision once it's bubbling away, making this perfect for a lazy afternoon of pottering around while filling your kitchen with clouds of balmy miso. It's great both as a warming snack, or with a bowl of rice for a fuller meal.

Put the ribs, garlic, ginger and dashi in a large saucepan. Bring to the boil, then reduce the heat to a simmer and cook for 2 hours. Skim off any impurities every 30 minutes, to leave a clear broth. Next add the carrot and daikon and cook until tender (this should take 15–20 minutes).

Now make sure that the dashi is on a gentle simmer, reducing the heat if necessary. Place both types of miso in a ladle or sieve (strainer). Dip the ladle or sieve into the saucepan so the dashi seeps in, but the miso does not escape into the pot. Slowly loosen up the miso with a spoon inside the ladle or sieve as the dashi mixes with it; the paste will slowly melt into the dashi.

Turn off the heat. Remove the ribs from the pot and quickly strip the pork from the bones, then return the meat to the broth. Sprinkle with the spring onion and serve, gently reheating the soup if necessary.

CHILLED MISO SOUP WITH CRAYFISH, CUCUMBER AND SESAME

SERVES 4

50 g/1¾ oz white miso
1 tbsp red miso
2 tbsp mirin
1 litre/1¾ pints Dashi (see page 40)
150 g/5½ oz cooked crayfish (crawfish) tails
100 g/3½ oz cucumber
2 tbsp julienned carrot
1 tbsp finely chopped fresh chives
1 tsp toasted sesame seeds
chilli (chile) oil (optional)

TIP: Do make sure that this soup is thoroughly chilled for a refreshing taste; this can take up to 4 hours, or overnight for best results. Use lightly poached prawns (shrimp) if you cannot get hold of crayfish.

I don't normally recommend cold miso soup – by which I mean miso soup that has gone cold like a forgotten cup of tea – but this deliberately chilled soup is so refreshing on a hot summer's day or a warm evening. I remember trying it for the first time on an unbearable August day in Tokyo, where the heat had taken away my appetite and I was looking for something tasty and cooling to eat that didn't involve ice cream. It was this soup that got my tastebuds going again; rarely does a chilled soup have this much depth of flavour. Served on its own as a snack, or with a warm bowl of rice for a light dinner, this is a soup to have on standby during the warmer months.

First, mix the miso pastes and mirin in a small bowl until smooth.

Pour the dashi into a saucepan and bring to the boil, then reduce the heat to a simmer. Add the crayfish and cook for 1 minute.

Turn off the heat. Dip a ladle containing the miso mixture into the pot so the dashi seeps in, but the miso does not escape into the pot. Slowly loosen up the miso with a spoon inside the ladle as the dashi mixes with it; the paste will slowly melt into the dashi.

Leave to cool to room temperature for 1 hour, then chill for a minimum of 2 hours, or overnight if possible.

When ready to serve, with a vegetable peeler, peel the cucumber into ribbons. Divide these between 4 bowls, then pour in the miso soup with the crayfish. The soup will have separated while in the refrigerator and this is normal; just give it a vigorous stir to bring it back together again.

Add the carrot, chives, sesame seeds and a few drops of chilli oil, if using, then serve.

WILD MUSHROOM AND BARLEY MISO SOUP

SERVES 4

- 1 litre/1¾ pints Dashi (see page 40)
- 50 g/1¾ oz small pearl onions, peeled but left whole
- 150 g/5½ oz wild mushrooms, ideally oyster or shiitake, or chestnut (cremini) mushrooms
- 85 g/3 oz barley miso
- 1 tbsp finely chopped coriander (cilantro) leaves (optional)

For me, barley miso ticks all my boxes. For classic miso soup, you need to use a blend of white and red miso for a balanced result, but when you use barley miso, it is already complete; socks on, ready to go. Its sweet winey notes blend effortlessly with the deep flavours that come from its longer ferment (usually 12–18 months). The distinctively nutty taste, pumpkin colours and grainy barley pieces give this soup a particularly autumnal vibe that loves wild mushrooms, herbs and even gamey meats. If I am craving miso soup and in a hurry, I tend to grab barley miso, knowing it's perfectly balanced and will go well with any sort of mushrooms or vegetables I have kicking around.

First, heat the dashi in a saucepan to a rolling boil and cook the pearl onions in it for 10–15 minutes until tender.

Clean and roughly slice the mushrooms, add them to the hot dashi and cook for 3–4 minutes until tender. Reduce the heat to a low simmer.

Place the miso in a ladle or sieve (strainer). Dip the ladle or sieve into the saucepan so the dashi seeps in, but the miso does not escape into the pot. Turn the heat off.

Slowly loosen up the miso with a spoon inside the ladle or sieve as the dashi mixes with it; the paste will slowly melt into the dashi. Ladle the mushrooms, onions and broth into bowls and sprinkle with coriander, if using, before serving.

OZONI

KYOTO NEW YEAR MISO SOUP

SERVES 4

1 litre/1¾ pints Dashi (see page 40), or vegetable stock
1 carrot, peeled and sliced into rounds, or cut into flower shapes
150 g/5½ oz daikon, peeled and cut into rounds
100 g/3½ oz silken tofu, finely chopped
70–85 g/2½–3 oz *saikyo* sweet white miso, or 70 g/2½ oz white miso plus 2 tsp caster (superfine) sugar
4 mochi cakes

New Year celebrations in Japan are really special. I have spent many dawns of a new calendar year in Kyoto, Japan's ancient capital. While the traditions are charming, old habits die hard and the hangover I suffer the morning after is always punishing. Thankfully, miso has the remedy.

Miso is known for its ability to cure a hangover by replacing lost salts and supporting detox of the liver, and, while I don't think this traditional miso soup was designed with that in mind, it sure is welcome! Miso soup is great for settling an upset stomach too and can return you back to the land of the living within a few sips.

Ozoni is enjoyed on the morning of New Year's Day and is unique in that it uses only sweet white *saikyo* miso, which famously hails from Kyoto. It also contains mochi, a fluffy pillow cake made from glutinous rice, which can be bought from all Japanese food shops. This is a soothing miso soup, sweet with custard notes: a gentle way to bring in the New Year.

Preheat the oven to 140°C fan/160°C/325°F/gas mark 3.

Pour the dashi into a saucepan, bring to a simmer, then drop in the carrot and daikon and cook until tender (about 5 minutes). Remove the vegetables with a slotted spoon and set aside, then skim any impurities from the surface of the broth.

Add the tofu to the broth and warm through for 1 minute.

Place the miso paste into a ladle and suspend it in the surface of the broth, stirring with a spoon. As *saikyo* miso is softer in texture than other types, it melts easily into the dashi.

Place the mochi cakes in the oven to puff up, which takes about 3 minutes, before adding to the soup. You will be amazed by how big these rice cakes can grow!

Divide the vegetables between 4 bowls, pour over the miso soup and finish each with a freshly toasted mochi on top.

GINDARA SAIKYOZUKE

MISO BLACK COD

SERVES 4

- 1 tbsp soy sauce
- 200 g/7 oz *saikyo* miso, or white miso
- 1 tbsp finely grated lemon zest
- 4 tbsp sake
- 4 tbsp mirin
- 3 tbsp caster (superfine) sugar
- 4 skin-on fillets of black cod (or see recipe introduction)

Often one of the fanciest miso dishes on the menu, this was made famous in the 1980s by the celebrated chef Nobu Matsuhisa. Thanks to its hefty price tag in restaurants, it is one of my most requested recipes for cooks looking to recreate the flavours at home. I get it. I remember the first time I tasted this: the creamy fish melted in my mouth. Just thinking about its butteriness makes my mouth water.

Confusingly, black cod is not a type of cod. It is actually from a different family of fish and its proper name is sablefish. Making this dish with cod fillets will not give you the same rich oily textures. Since sablefish is only available in the icy waters of the Pacific North West, I buy it online and it arrives frozen. If you don't want to do the same, I recommend you choose a thick cod loin; the loin is from the middle third section of the cod and is moist and flaky. Or choose a fish with a similar texture and richness, such as mackerel, trout or red snapper.

In a small bowl, combine the soy sauce, miso and lemon zest and mix until smooth.

In a small saucepan, heat the sake and mirin over a high heat for 30 seconds to evaporate the alcohol. Then reduce the heat and whisk in the miso mixture until smooth. Increase the heat again and add the sugar, but be careful it doesn't burn. Turn off the heat and leave to cool to room temperature.

Put the fish in a bowl. Smother both sides of each fillet generously with the cold miso mixture, then cover the bowl and refrigerate. Leave to marinate for at least 3 hours, or overnight, or up to 3 days, if you have the time.

When ready to cook, preheat the grill (broiler) to medium and preheat the oven to 150°C fan/170°C/340°F/gas mark 3. Wipe off any excess miso clinging to the fish.

Grill the fish, about 7.5 cm/3 in from the grill, skin side up first, for 3 minutes, until you see bubbles and a little charring.

Transfer to the oven and bake for 7–10 minutes until the fish is opaque and flakes easily. It will be just cooked and tender on the inside. Serve immediately with rice and simple steamed or stir-fried greens.

NASU DENGAKU

MISO AUBERGINE

SERVES 4

2 aubergines (eggplants)
8 tbsp olive oil, plus more if needed
75 g/2¾ oz white miso
20 ml/¾ fl oz mirin
10 g/¼ oz caster (superfine) sugar
1 spring onion (scallion), finely chopped
toasted sesame seeds, to serve (optional)

This will convert even the most committed aubergine-sceptic. Creamy and umami-rich, sweet and succulent, this classic dish has become incredibly popular outside Japan over the last few years and is always a crowd-pleaser. It is one of my most frequent go-to dishes when cooking for friends, especially a mixed group of vegetarians and omnivores, when I want to make something just as satisfying for both. I have made this hundreds of times and have honed my recipe over the years to have far fewer ingredients than the original version, to keep it as simple as possible, because I want it to be on your weekly rota!

It is easy to make good miso aubergine, but it takes a bit of experience to make an outstanding miso aubergine. Here are my tips for god-tier miso aubergines every time.

1. Do not skimp on the oil. This is not a time for calorie-counting. Slather the scored aubergine with oil, then add some more. This both speeds up the cooking and converts squeaky aubergine into creamy aubergine: you should be able to slice through the whole vegetable easily once cooked through, with no chewiness. Check the aubergines halfway through cooking to see if they need an oil top-up, too.

2. Make sure your aubergines are *fully* cooked through, before adding the glaze. The number one mistake I have seen in other versions of this dish is cooks adding the glaze to *raw* aubergine: the glaze will burn before the aubergine is cooked.

3. Only grill or roast the aubergine with the glaze for five minutes, or until bubbly and golden. More than this and the sauce starts to dry out too much, or worse, burn.

We don't always have time to bake whole aubergines in this way, so I have also given you two other variations (see pages 61–63), both of which take less time to make and are great for midweek dinners.

Continues overleaf

TIP: BAKED MISO AUBERGINE MEDALLIONS
Instead of roasting aubergine (eggplant) halves, which takes more time, you can simply slice an aubergine widthways to create medallions, then score the top part of the slices in a criss-cross pattern, to help the oil to seep into the flesh more quickly. These need to bake for just 12 minutes. The rest of the dish remains the same: paint the sauce on the aubergine slices and roast for a further 5 minutes until golden. This more than halves the cooking time and makes miso aubergines a more shareable dish, or a speedy working-from-home lunch.

Preheat the oven to 180°C fan/200°C/400°F/gas mark 6.

Halve the aubergines lengthways and score the flesh with a sharp knife in a criss-cross. Go as deep as you can into the aubergine flesh without piercing through the skin on the base.

Drizzle generously with the oil and place on a baking tray lined with baking paper (parchment paper). Bake for at least 20 minutes, until fully cooked through (see recipe introduction). Check halfway through to see if there are any bits of aubergine that need an extra drizzle of oil to help them cook through fully. When they are ready, the aubergines will be puckered up with the criss-cross slices spreading out, golden on top, and the flesh will be juicy and moist right down to the baking tray. If they need more time, return them to the oven, checking every 5 minutes.

In a small bowl, mix together the miso, mirin and sugar, then loosen the sauce with 1–2 tsp of room-temperature water. Using a brush or spoon, spread the sauce over the aubergine in a 3–4 mm/¼ in layer on top, making sure you take it to the edges of the halved aubergines.

Put the aubergines back in the oven for a further 5–7 minutes: the sauce will be bubbling, golden and sticky. If you like it more charred, then pop under a hot grill (broiler) for an extra minute before serving.

Serve half an aubergine per person, scattered with the spring onion and sesame seeds. Delicious with plain rice and salad.

SPICY FRIED MISO AUBERGINES

SERVES 4

5 tbsp olive oil, plus more if needed
2 small chillies (chiles), finely chopped
2 garlic cloves, finely chopped
2 large aubergines (eggplants), chopped into 2.5 cm/1 in cubes
50 g/1¾ oz red miso
3 tbsp sake
3 tbsp toasted sesame oil
3 tbsp mirin
2 tbsp caster (superfine) sugar
1 spring onion (scallion), finely chopped
1 tbsp chopped coriander (cilantro) leaves (optional)

You can also make miso aubergines (eggplants) on the stove. In this recipe, you chop your aubergines into cubes and sauté with olive oil until totally cooked through. It will take around 15 minutes, and don't be afraid to add more oil if the aubergines are not cooking through. They should be soft and juicy, without any squeaky textures when you taste them.

First heat the oil in a large saucepan or wok over a high heat. Add one of the chopped chillies and all the garlic and stir-fry for 1 minute. Add the aubergines, 2 handfuls at a time, stir-frying each batch for 3–5 minutes until cooked through and tender. Some aubergines absorb more oil than others, so have some extra oil on standby, in case you need it.

In a small mixing bowl, mix the miso, sake, sesame oil, mirin and sugar until you have a thick, smooth sauce.

Once all the aubergines are cooked, return them all to the pan, then reduce the heat to medium before pouring the miso sauce over. Stir for 3–4 minutes until heated through and the aubergines have started to absorb the sauce. Add the second chopped chilli and the spring onion and cook for a further minute. Sprinkle with the coriander, if you like, then serve.

RAFUTE

OKINAWAN PORK BELLY

SERVES 4–6

70 g/2½ oz red miso
2 tbsp sake
3 tbsp mirin
2 tbsp soy sauce
900 g/2 lb pork belly
3 tbsp olive oil
15 cm/6 in daikon, cut into 5 cm/2 in cubes
1 large carrot, cut into 2.5 cm/1 in cubes
1 litre/1¾ pints hot water
2 tbsp sweet white miso
finely chopped spring onions (scallions), to serve (optional)

TIP: If you have any broth left over, I highly recommend throwing some noodles into it the next day for a rich tonkotsu-style ramen, so you can enjoy at least two meals out of this.

I spent a long break in Okinawa and it remains one of the most peaceful trips of my life. I was lured in by the mystique of its status as the number one Blue Zone in the world, with three times the number of centenarians per 100,000 inhabitants than the US. Naturally, I was curious to know what the locals were eating to grant them such long lives. On menus, I saw a lot of bitter melon, eggs, tofu, miso... and then pork belly, bacon and Spam! These porky additions were a surprise, but I suppose the proof is in the people's longevity.

This dish contains two types of miso: a deep red miso for the marinade and for cooking, then a sweet white miso to mellow out the rich broth. It requires overnight marinating, but actually very little attention once everything is in the pot. Just return two hours later for a rich reward.

In a small mixing bowl, combine the miso, sake, mirin and soy sauce to create a marinade. Slice the pork belly into 5 cm/2 in cubes and place in a bowl, rub the marinade over them, cover and leave overnight in the refrigerator.

The next day, brown the pork belly in a hot dry frying pan (skillet) without oil, reserving the marinade, until the edges begin to darken and crisp up.

In a large casserole (Dutch oven), heat up the olive oil and cook the daikon and carrot for 2–3 minutes until slightly softened. Add the pork belly and all the leftover marinade, then pour in the measured hot water.

Cook over a low heat for 1½–2 hours until fully softened and melting away. Keep checking the pot every 30 minutes, giving it a quick stir to prevent anything sticking. In the last 5 minutes of cooking, place the sweet white miso in a ladle or sieve (strainer) and dip it into the hot pot, so the sauce seeps in but the miso does not escape into the pot. Loosen up the miso with a spoon inside the ladle or sieve; the paste will slowly melt into the dish. Cook for the final 5 minutes.

Sprinkle with the spring onions, if using, and serve with plenty of plain steamed rice and some stir-fried kale or Savoy cabbage.

HOW TO BUILD A RAMEN

Ramen is traditionally made with a pork or chicken bone broth called tonkotsu, but around Japan, you will also find different bases. Tokyo-style ramen has a soy sauce-based broth, for instance, which is less heavy. Miso-based ramen often still includes the pork bone base. I found the widest choice of miso ramen when travelling around Hokkaido, the northern island of Japan. If you are vegetarian, it can be tricky to find miso ramen without meat or fish as a stock base, so do your research before you go. Below is my all-purpose quick miso ramen formula, naturally vegetarian, with miso as its base. Add any toppings you desire: this is a great home for leftover roast meats and fish. Aim to use one protein and a couple of vegetables, for a balanced meal.

VARIATIONS

1. To make miso ramen creamier, swap half the dashi with soya milk and add a knob of butter on top to serve.

2. To make miso ramen more traditional, replace the vegetarian dashi with a mixture of pork stock and bonito dashi (see page 40).

1. DASHI BASE

First, make 400 ml/14 fl oz of dashi per portion, made from kombu, shiitake mushrooms and bonito flakes (optional). See page 40 for my Dashi recipe. Or you can use instant powdered dashi – check it doesn't contain artificial flavourings.

2. BLEND OF MISO PASTES

Stir the miso pastes into the dashi. Per portion you will need 1 tbsp of light miso paste and 1 tbsp of dark miso paste, plus 1 tbsp of sesame oil for added richness. You can also play with the ratios: the more dark miso you include in the blend, the richer the soup will taste.

3. RAMEN

Into the miso + dashi, add 140–180 g of cooked noodles per portion made according to packet instructions. Choose wheat-based noodles, without egg.

4. TOPPINGS

Finally, top your ramen!

1 x PROTEIN
Eggs, ham, roast meats, tofu, white and oily fish

2 x VEG
Seaweed, sautéed vegetables such as mushrooms, kale, carrots, sweetcorn, courgette (zucchini), mangetout (snow peas), beansprouts

1 x GARNISH
Finely sliced spring onions (scallions), a drizzle of garlic or chilli (chile) oil, pickles such as kimchi

SAPPORO RAMEN

SERVES 4

4 skin-on boneless chicken thighs
1 tbsp toasted sesame oil, plus 2 tsp to serve
1 tbsp light soy sauce
3 tbsp olive oil
1 small leek, peeled and finely chopped
1 carrot, peeled and julienned
2 heads of pak choi (bok choy), leaves halved lengthways
200 g/7 oz beansprouts
200 g/7 oz dried ramen noodles
1 litre/1¾ pints chicken stock
50 g/1¾ oz white miso
2 tbsp red miso
2 spring onions (scallions), finely shredded
100 g/3½ oz canned or fresh sweetcorn
60 g/2¼ oz unsalted butter, split into 4 even pieces
4 boiled eggs
a few drops of chilli (chile) oil (optional)
sea salt and freshly ground white pepper

This famous noodle soup hails from Sapporo, the capital of Japan's most northern island, Hokkaido. I was originally taken there to watch a rugby game, but stayed for the buttery food, bakeries and seafood. Their dishes are typically fatty and warming; a necessity for the harsh winters. This is a gutsy, pulls-no-punches kind of noodle soup, so make sure you are hungry! The sweetcorn and butter toppings are its hallmarks, as the island is known for producing the sweetest corn and renowned for its local dairy.

First, rub the chicken with the 1 tbsp sesame oil and the light soy sauce. Heat up the olive oil in a frying pan (skillet). Add the chicken, skin side down, and fry until crisp on the skin, about 3 minutes, then flip over and cook for a further 4 minutes until tender and cooked through. Remove the chicken from the pan and leave to cool.

Add the vegetables to the same pan (except the spring onions and sweetcorn) and stir-fry for 5 minutes with some salt and white pepper.

Separately, in a large pot of hot water, cook the noodles according to the packet instructions. Once cooked, drain them under very cold water to stop the cooking process, then divide between 4 bowls.

Pour the chicken stock into a saucepan and bring to the boil for 3 minutes, then reduce the heat to a simmer. Place both types of miso in a ladle or sieve (strainer). Dip the ladle or sieve into the saucepan so the stock seeps in, but the miso does not escape into the pot. Slowly loosen up the miso with a spoon inside the ladle or sieve as the stock mixes with it; the paste will slowly melt into the dish.

Slice the chicken thighs, lay them with the vegetables in the bowls on top of the noodles, then ladle the hot miso stock on top. Divide the spring onions, sweetcorn and butter between each bowl, adding a boiled egg, sliced in half, and sprinkling with the 2 tsp sesame oil and some chilli oil, if you like, then serve immediately.

TOFU DENGAKU

GRILLED TOFU WITH MISO LEEK SAUCE

SERVES 4 AS A STARTER (APPETIZER) OR A SIDE DISH

70 g/2½ oz white miso
2 tbsp mirin
1 tsp toasted sesame oil
2 tbsp caster (superfine) sugar
2 tbsp water
1 tbsp olive oil
100 g/3½ oz leeks, finely chopped
300 g/10½ oz firm tofu, drained
spring onion (scallion) greens, shredded, to serve

TIP: For a stronger flavour, swap the white miso for barley miso, or for a blend of red and white miso. The miso sauce is also great for dipping raw celery or daikon, for a snack.

Something about their beany companionship makes miso and tofu a perfect and frequent pairing in Japanese cooking. Miso absorbs quickly into tofu and injects it with a huge hit of flavour. This dish is very quick to make, as the tofu absorbs its marinade thoroughly within an hour. The fried leeks bring a smoky sweetness which makes the dish so tasty that it can be eaten on its own.

This recipe is inspired by the traditional *dengaku* technique, in which tofu or vegetables are skewered like kebabs and grilled with a sweet miso sauce.

To make the marinade, mix the miso, mirin and sesame oil to a smooth paste in a small saucepan, before stirring in the sugar and measured water. Cook over a low heat for 2 minutes until the sauce has thickened.

Heat the olive oil in a separate frying pan (skillet) set over a medium heat, then sauté the leeks for 2 minutes until softened. Cool completely before adding to the miso marinade.

Preheat the grill (broiler) to medium.

Cut the tofu into domino-sized pieces, each 1 cm/½ in thick, and place on a baking tray lined with foil. Put under the grill for 1 minute on each side. Now take the pieces out and brush with the miso marinade.

Place the tofu back under the grill for a further 2 minutes. Watch carefully, as the sauce – with its sugar and miso – can burn quickly. Sprinkle with shredded spring onions to finish, if you like.

FUROFUKI DAIKON

SIMMERED DAIKON WITH MISO MUSTARD SAUCE

SERVES 4 AS A STARTER (APPETIZER) OR SIDE DISH

- 500 ml/18 fl oz Dashi (see page 40)
- 30 cm/12 in daikon, peeled and sliced into 1.5 cm-/5/8 in-thick rounds
- 3 tsp French wholegrain mustard
- 1½ tbsp mirin
- 1 tsp olive oil
- 1 tsp toasted sesame oil
- 2 tbsp white miso
- 1 tsp finely grated lemon zest

TIP: This sauce is also great as a dip for fish and seafood, especially cooked prawns (shrimp) and seared tuna.

Daikon in Japanese, 'mooli' in Hindi and 'white carrots' in Chinese, these large radishes are enjoyed across Asia. They are simple to cook and have an inherent sweet flavour, all held together by a porous structure that loves to take on flavoursome sauces. Here, daikon is simmered until cooked through and then finished with an addictive topping of miso and mustard; a spiky shot of flavour that is calmed by the soothing simmered lily pad of daikon underneath.

Pour the dashi into a saucepan and bring to the boil. Leave it to bubble for 5 minutes, then reduce the heat to a simmer, add the daikon slices and cook for 20 minutes until they appear almost translucent. You will be able to put a fork through a slice easily. Leave the daikon and dashi to cool.

Spoon 3 tbsp of the cooled dashi into a separate saucepan over a medium heat and add the mustard, mirin, and olive and sesame oils.

At the last minute, stir in the miso paste for 2 minutes until fully mixed together, then take off the heat. Spoon the miso mustard mix over each piece of daikon and sprinkle the lemon zest on the top for its colour and flavour.

HOW TO BUILD A YAKI UDON

Yaki udon is available everywhere in Japan; served in *izakayas* (Japanese pubs), at *imatsuri* (festivals) and at street-side vendors. At home, it is a thrifty, satisfying midweek meal in minutes. Yaki means grilled (broiled), so a good yaki udon should have a lick of char about it, sometimes even with a few burnt bits. It is rough-and-ready comfort food.

To recreate this at home, here is a guide to getting it right every time. It looks like a very simple dish, but these little tips will elevate your yaki udon to another level.

1 You can get straight-to-wok udon noodles and these are fine to use for this dish. However, frozen udon noodles take it to another level, with a chewy, bouncy texture that is super-satisfying.

2 The temptation is to load your pan with lots of vegetables and protein, but remember that the udon is the star here, so let it sing: less is more. You want the miso sauce to coat every noodle strand, so pick one protein and one or two vegetables only: more than this and the sauce will cling on to everything apart from the noodles.

3 This dish comes together super-quickly, so the key is to have everything chopped and ready to go, with the sauce mixed.

4 Avoid using a non-stick pan, as you want the noodles to catch on the high heat and char slightly. Traditionally, yaki udon is cooked on a flat teppanyaki grill, like a hot plate, so don't be afraid to pump up the heat if you only have a non-stick pan.

5 Once you have poured the sauce over the noodles, resist the temptation to move anything in the pan, just patiently let the flavours soak in. As the sauce thickens, the flavours will intensify. At most, you can flip your noodles twice towards the end of cooking.

6 If you are cooking for quite a few people, I recommend making only two portions in the pan at a time. This is because any crowding in the pan will cause the noodles to steam to a mushy texture and prevent you from achieving that sticky, slightly crispy texture that is the hallmark of a great yaki udon.

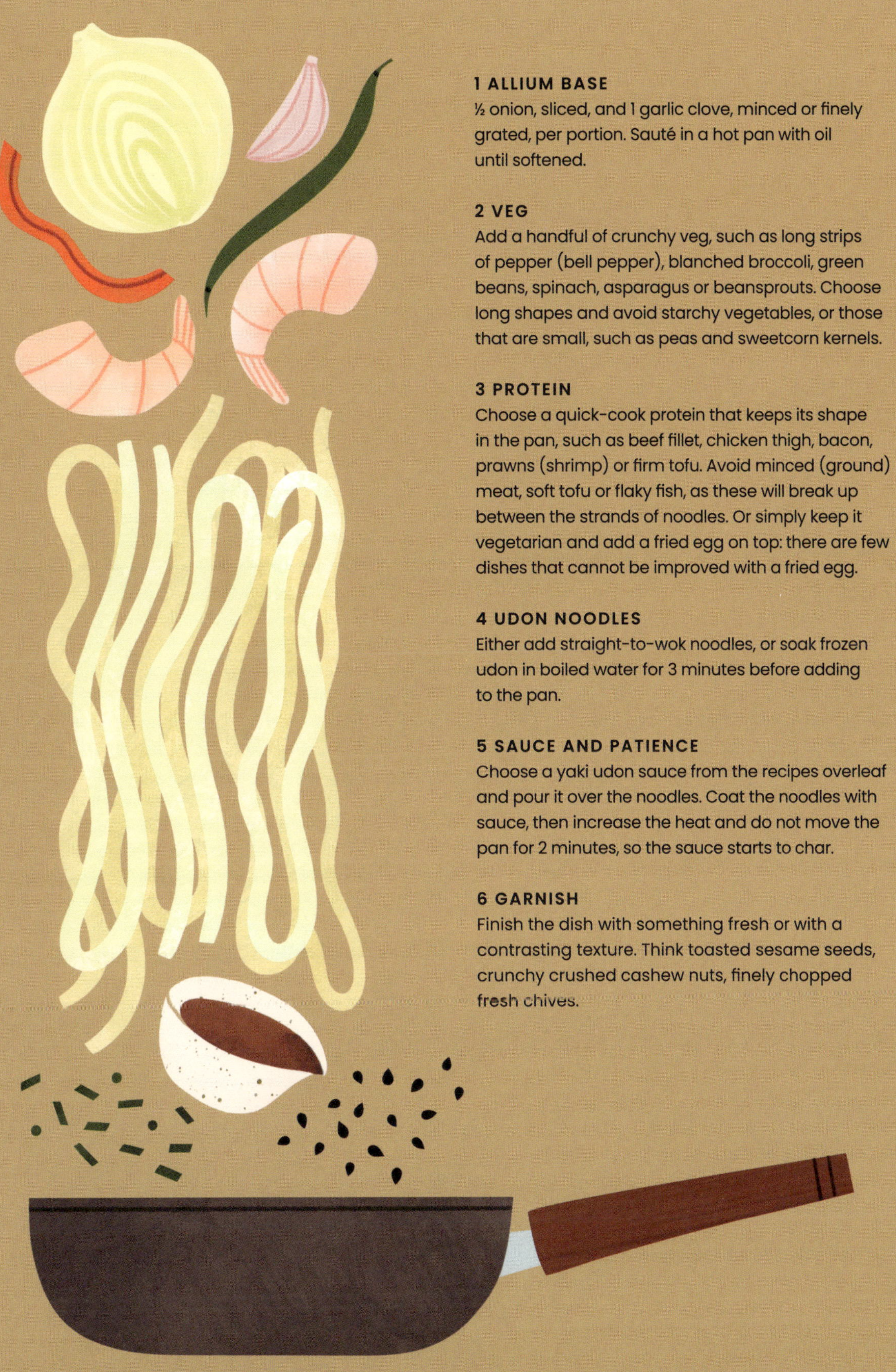

1 ALLIUM BASE

½ onion, sliced, and 1 garlic clove, minced or finely grated, per portion. Sauté in a hot pan with oil until softened.

2 VEG

Add a handful of crunchy veg, such as long strips of pepper (bell pepper), blanched broccoli, green beans, spinach, asparagus or beansprouts. Choose long shapes and avoid starchy vegetables, or those that are small, such as peas and sweetcorn kernels.

3 PROTEIN

Choose a quick-cook protein that keeps its shape in the pan, such as beef fillet, chicken thigh, bacon, prawns (shrimp) or firm tofu. Avoid minced (ground) meat, soft tofu or flaky fish, as these will break up between the strands of noodles. Or simply keep it vegetarian and add a fried egg on top: there are few dishes that cannot be improved with a fried egg.

4 UDON NOODLES

Either add straight-to-wok noodles, or soak frozen udon in boiled water for 3 minutes before adding to the pan.

5 SAUCE AND PATIENCE

Choose a yaki udon sauce from the recipes overleaf and pour it over the noodles. Coat the noodles with sauce, then increase the heat and do not move the pan for 2 minutes, so the sauce starts to char.

6 GARNISH

Finish the dish with something fresh or with a contrasting texture. Think toasted sesame seeds, crunchy crushed cashew nuts, finely chopped fresh chives.

YAKI UDON SAUCES

Udon *loves* the contrast of sweetness, spice and acidity and so the design of all three of my go-to yaki udon sauces is built on the Sa-Shi-Su-Se-So principle (see page 38). Red miso is used in all of them, as the oiliness of the dish and the plain nature of udon can stand up to it. You can also enjoy these sauces in other stir-fries too. And to make the sauces vegan, swap the honey for maple syrup.

In each case, simply mix everything in a bowl until smooth. They all make enough sauce for two portions of noodles.

THE SWEET AND SOUR ONE

50 g/1¾ oz red miso
4 tbsp mirin
2 tbsp runny honey
2 tsp toasted sesame oil
4 tsp rice vinegar

This works well with chicken, tofu and vegetables.

THE SMOKY SPICY ONE

50 g/1¾ oz red miso
2 tbsp runny honey
2 tbsp chipotle paste
1 tbsp rice vinegar

Great with seafood, chicken and beef.

THE WARM AND PEPPERY ONE

50 g/1¾ oz red miso
4 tsp dark soy sauce
2 tsp freshly crushed or ground black peppercorns
2 tbsp runny honey
2 tsp rice vinegar

A good match with beef, lamb and tofu.

BUTAMISO UDON

UDON NOODLE SOUP WITH MISO PORK TOPPING

SERVES 4

500 g/1 lb 2 oz boneless pork shoulder
4 tbsp sake
2 tbsp *hatcho* (pure soya bean) miso
1 tbsp red miso
1 tbsp mirin
2 tbsp brown sugar
a little olive oil
3 spring onions (scallions), finely chopped
50 g/1¾ oz daikon, finely chopped, plus 1 tbsp grated daikon to serve
2 garlic cloves, finely chopped
1 tbsp peeled and finely grated root ginger
200 g/7 oz dried udon noodles, or 4 packs of frozen udon
1 litre/1¾ pints Dashi (see page 40)

This super-versatile porky miso sauce is really addictive; it's like the bolognese of Japan. Fatty and full of flavour, it can go on top of almost any starchy foods. To add a bit of texture, I include finely chopped daikon to the mix too. Fattier pork shoulder is much better than lean pork here. This recipe makes more pork sauce than you will need, but it keeps in the refrigerator for a week, or freezes well, and is fantastic on top of rice or potatoes, stir-fried with greens, or as a snack with cucumber batons.

First mince (grind) the pork shoulder, either with a food processor or by hand; the latter gives a much more textured finish. Place the meat in a bowl with 1 tbsp of the sake and mix well.

Pour the rest of the sake into a small mixing bowl with both types of miso, the mirin and brown sugar. Give it a good mix, until the sauce is smooth.

Put the oil in a frying pan (skillet) over a medium heat. Once hot, add 2 of the finely chopped spring onions, the chopped daikon and the garlic for 30 seconds. Add the pork and stir until it is no longer pink; this takes about 3 minutes.

Add the miso mixture to the pan and stir for a further 2 minutes before adding the ginger. Let cool to room temperature.

In a large saucepan, cook the udon noodles in the dashi according to the packet instructions. Drain, reserving the dashi, cool the noodles under cold water to stop them cooking further, then divide between 4 bowls.

Skim off any impurities from the dashi, return to the boil, then pour over the noodles.

Add 3 tbsp of the miso pork topping to each bowl. Sprinkle each with the grated daikon and the remaining spring onion and serve.

ZARU SOBA

CHILLED SOBA NOODLES WITH MISO SESAME DIPPING SAUCE

SERVES 4

250 g/9 oz toasted sesame seeds
100 g/3½ oz caster (superfine) sugar
100 g/3½ oz white miso
4 tsp soy sauce
2 tsp toasted sesame oil
100 ml/3½ fl oz water
400 g/14 oz soba noodles
100 g/3½ oz spring onions (scallions), finely sliced

Every time I make this dipping sauce, I berate myself for not making more… I just can't get enough! With this dish you need little else, but I find simple wilted spinach or green beans pair deliciously.

This is a refreshing meal when it's warm outside, perfect for taking into work and keeping in the refrigerator until lunchtime, or as a weekend lunch alongside other light dishes. The cool noodles are dipped into the sesame sauce before slurping. Divine!

In a large saucepan, bring some water to the boil.

Meanwhile, using a mortar and pestle, or, even better, a Japanese suribachi – which is similar but with grooves for extra friction – grind the sesame seeds until you have a paste. This can take up to 10 minutes. If you have a spice or coffee grinder, that works, too.

Next, add the sugar and combine with the sesame seeds.

Turn out the sweet sesame paste into a bowl and work in the miso, soy sauce and sesame oil. Gradually add the measured water until the sauce has the consistency of salad dressing.

When the saucepan of water boils, add the soba noodles and cook according to the packet instructions. Drain them in a sieve (strainer) and rinse under cold running water until completely cold. Add some ice cubes to cool them down further.

When ready to serve, divide the miso-sesame sauce between 4 dipping bowls and serve the noodles on the side. For every mouthful, simply dip the noodles and spring onions into the sauce to enjoy. The sauce also makes a great salad dressing, if you have any left over.

DONBURI GYUDON

SIMMERED MISO BEEF AND ONION

SERVES 4

500 ml/18 fl oz beef stock
2 tbsp sake
3 tbsp mirin
2 tbsp caster (superfine) sugar
1 onion, finely sliced
250 g/9 oz short-grain Japanese rice (if unavailable, try jasmine rice)
300 g/10½ oz beef for *shabu shabu* (beef with deep marbling, thinly sliced)
45 g/1½ oz red miso
4 eggs
1 tbsp light-coloured vinegar, such as white wine vinegar, or rice vinegar

TIP: For successful poached eggs, make sure you have fresh eggs: more than a week old and the whites do not hold together as well.

Donburi **is a one-bowl comfort dish of fluffy boiled rice topped with simmered savoury ingredients, including meat, vegetables or seafood. In this recipe, miso brings a caramelized note to slow-cooked silvery strands of onions and beef, for a quick and hearty midweek meal. You can add pickles or a side of vegetables, too.**

First, bring the stock to the boil in a saucepan and add the sake, mirin and sugar. Reduce the heat to a simmer, add the onion and cook for a further 10 minutes to soften.

Meanwhile, wash the rice and set it to cook in a separate saucepan according to the packet instructions.

Add the beef to the simmering onion for a further 10 minutes.

In a small bowl, mix the miso paste with a ladle of the cooking liquid from the beef and onions, stirring until smooth with no lumps, then pour back into the pot and simmer very gently for another 5 minutes.

When the rice is ready, leave to cool slightly, while you poach the eggs. For me, the keys to achieving perfect poached eggs are some light vinegar, a fine-meshed sieve, a deep saucepan and a little bowl or ramekin. Fill a deep saucepan with water and bring to the boil. (A sauté pan also works, but will give you a flatter egg.) Add the vinegar.

Crack each egg into a fine mesh sieve over a small bowl to get rid of some of the watery egg white; this helps to bind the poached egg. Carefully transfer the egg to a ramekin.

Reduce the heat under the water to a very low simmer and pour in the egg, which will at first dive to the bottom and then slowly rise again. Set the timer for 3 minutes. Remove with a slotted spoon, then dab gently with kitchen paper (paper towel) to remove excess water.

Divide the rice between 4 bowls, pouring the miso beef and onion topping over and placing a runny poached egg in the centre. Each diner should mix everything together before devouring.

24-HOUR MISO-MARINATED PORK SHOULDER STEAKS

SERVES 4

120 g/4 oz white miso
2 tbsp toasted sesame oil
2 tbsp sake
3 tbsp mirin
1 tbsp soy sauce
1 tbsp brown sugar
1 garlic clove, finely chopped
1 tbsp peeled and finely chopped or grated root ginger
4 pork shoulder steaks, each 150 g/5½ oz
a little flavourless oil

I have always reserved pork shoulder for slow cooking and stews, but a new revelation has been enjoying pork shoulder steaks as if they were pork chops. The fatty marbling gives a juicy texture throughout, an area in which pork chops often fail. The long marinade here also helps to tenderize the meat, as well as coddling it while cooking so the moisture is locked inside. This is delicious with a green salad, served with rice, or as a topping for a bowl of steaming noodles.

Simply stir all the ingredients apart from the pork and flavourless oil in a mixing bowl, in the order in which they are listed, starting with the miso, then all the liquids, then the sugar, garlic and ginger at the end.

Pour the marinade over the pork, cover and refrigerate for 24 hours, or overnight.

When ready to cook, preheat the oven to 160°C fan/180°C/350°F/gas mark 4. Dab the pork gently with kitchen paper (paper towels) to remove any excess marinade.

Heat a frying pan (skillet). Fry the pork in the dry pan for 4 minutes on each side, then place in an oiled roasting tray and roast for 7 minutes until cooked through and tender.

GOMA MISO

CHARGRILLED TENDERSTEM BROCCOLI WITH SESAME MISO DRESSING

SERVES 4

---

300 g/10½ oz Tenderstem broccoli (broccolini), trimmed
1 tbsp olive oil
50 g/1¾ oz sesame seeds
1 tsp caster (superfine) sugar
2 tbsp sweet white miso, or white miso
1 tbsp mirin
4 tbsp water

A very popular home-style dish in Japan, the hero here is the sauce: *goma miso*. Drizzle this over any cooked green vegetables for a creamy, nutty topping. Keep a bottle of it in the refrigerator on standby to jazz up vegetables instantly. I love it on sugarsnap peas (snap peas), mangetout (snow peas), green beans and spinach too.

Preheat the oven to 140°C fan/160°C/325°F/gas mark 3.

Blanch the broccoli in a saucepan of boiling water for 3 minutes. Drain well, then toss with the olive oil.

Heat a griddle (grill) pan over a high heat and grill the broccoli for a further 2 minutes, then remove from the heat and leave to cool.

Tip the sesame seeds on to a baking sheet and roast in the oven for 5 minutes until golden, stirring gently to prevent them burning. Release their nutty aroma by crushing them with a mortar and pestle while they are still warm, adding the sugar. For the smoothest results, use a Japanese suribachi, where there are grooves on the inside of the bowl to help grind the seeds more quickly. (A spice grinder or coffee grinder will also work.)

Tip the sesame paste into a mixing bowl and work in the miso and mirin until fully combined. Finally add the measured water slowly, until you have a thick sauce. (You may not need it all.)

Once the broccoli has cooled to room temperature, pour over the sauce.

CHANKO NABE

THE SUMO WRESTLER'S HOT POT

SERVES 4

For the fish balls
300 g/10½ oz sardine fillets
2.5 cm/1 in root ginger, peeled and finely grated
2 tbsp white miso
bunch of fresh chives, chopped
1 tbsp plain (all-purpose) flour

For the hot pot
800 ml/1 pint 7 fl oz Dashi (see page 40)
150 ml/5 fl oz sake
1½ tbsp soy sauce
4 eggs
200 g/7 oz skinless boneless chicken, cut into cubes
1 daikon, peeled and chopped into 1 cm-/½ in-thick half-moons
12 fresh shiitake mushrooms
1 head of pak choi, trimmed, leaves halved lengthways
1 large leek, trimmed and finely sliced
200 g/7 oz firm tofu, cut into 1 cm/½ in cubes

TIP: To present this dish in the authentic way, set it on a portable stove over a very low heat at the centre of the table, giving guests individual bowls to serve themselves.

If you are cooking for a crowd, this is quite a centrepiece and the ultimate one-pot meal. *Chanko nabe* is part of the traditional diet of sumo wrestlers, hence its heartiness and multiple sources of protein. It forms the first meal of their day after a whole morning of exercise. This is a much lighter version, though loaded with chicken, fish, tofu and vegetables.

Miso here is featured in the fish balls, a signature part of the dish that has fuelled Japan's national sport for centuries.

First make the fish balls by putting all the ingredients into a food processor. Pulse-blend so that the texture is rough, not finely ground. Refrigerate the mix for 30 minutes.

In a large saucepan or casserole (Dutch oven), heat the dashi to boiling, then reduce the heat to a simmer. Drop large tablespoons of the fish ball mixture into the stock. They take 3–4 minutes to cook. Remove them from the heat and set aside.

Skim the stock to ensure any impurities are removed and it stays clear. Add the sake and soy sauce and simmer for 20 minutes.

Meanwhile, in a separate saucepan, boil the eggs for 6 minutes, then cool, peel and slice in half.

Add the chicken, daikon, shiitake, pak choi, leek and tofu to the broth and simmer for another 20 minutes until the chicken is cooked. When ready to serve, return the fish balls and simmer for a final 3 minutes. Serve in bowls, with the halved eggs.

TAMAGO MISOZUKE

MISO-CURED DUCK EGG YOLKS ON SHISO LEAVES

SERVES 4 AS AN APPETIZER

200 g/7 oz white miso
1½ tbsp sake
1½ tbsp caster (superfine) sugar
4 large duck egg yolks
4 shiso leaves

Here's one for the cooking geeks, though I take no credit for this amazing piece of food science alchemy. I first tried these many years ago at an *izakaya* (Japanese pub) in Ochanomizu, Tokyo, called Kagiroi, and I have been going back ever since to enjoy them. *Izakayas* are akin to gastropubs or tapas bars, evening drinking places, usually tiny, charming and open late, serving delicious morsels on small plates. It is hard to imagine a more fun way to spend time with friends.

Here, egg yolks are coddled in white miso for four days. By osmosis, the water is drawn out and the miso seeps in until the yolk is solid and full of umami flavour. In my recipe, I use large duck eggs for dramatic effect, but regular hen's eggs work in the same way.

In a mixing bowl, blend the miso, sake and sugar together.

Take 4 small coffee cups, teacups, or small bowls no wider than 5 cm/2 in in diameter. Line each with 1 sheet of kitchen paper (paper towel), which has been briefly soaked then squeezed of water and folded twice over into a square.

Drop 1 tbsp of the miso mixture into each lined cup and, using a small spoon, make a small hollow for an egg yolk to sit in. Drop the yolks into their wells. Cover each cup with clingfilm (plastic wrap) and leave in the refrigerator for 2 days.

Carefully turn each yolk over with a teaspoon, cover and return to the refrigerator for a further 3–4 days. The egg yolk will have become a bright orange colour and will be solid in texture.

Serve each yolk on top of a shiso leaf. Or they can be preserved for a further 10 days, if kept in an airtight box in the refrigerator.

TOFU MISOZUKE

MISO-CURED TOFU 'CHEESE'

MAKES ABOUT 200 G/7 OZ

180 g/6 oz firm tofu
145 g/5 oz white miso
1 tsp caster (superfine) sugar
1 tsp sake

It is amazing how frequently I am asked whether a miso dish contains cheese, when it doesn't. The familiar tangy, nutty sweet-and-salty flavours, aided by the lengthy fermentation process, does make miso surprisingly similar in taste to some cheeses.

Miso-cured tofu is a common product available from food halls across Japan. Enjoyed with toasted bread or crackers, its consistency is akin to a soft spreadable cheese, with a deep savoury taste. It's great as a vegan spread that's high in protein and natural flavour.

First, remove the water from the tofu by wrapping it in 2 layers of kitchen paper (paper towels) and placing it in a roasting or baking tin (pan). Place a plate on top of the tofu to act as a weight, followed by a bowl of ceramic baking beans or equivalent, for weight. This will push out the water from the tofu evenly. Leave for 30 minutes.

In a medium bowl, mix the miso, sugar and sake until smooth. Line a plastic box with 3 layers of kitchen paper and spread half the miso mixture along the base in the same dimensions as the tofu block. Sit the tofu on top.

Spread the rest of the miso along the sides and top of the tofu, then seal everything up with clingfilm (plastic wrap), including the kitchen paper.

After 2 days, you will have a lightly cured tofu to enjoy with toasted bread or crackers. For a deeper cure, change the kitchen paper and clingfilm and refresh the miso mixture once a month for up to 1 year, for the texture of matured cheese.

Like cheese, miso-cured tofu pairs very well with sweet and sharp pickles, chutneys and relishes, and, of course, a glass of wine.

TSUKEMONO

MISO PICKLED CUCUMBER

MAKES 1 JAM JAR FULL

6 small cucumbers
150 g/5½ oz red miso
150 g/5½ oz white miso
1 tbsp sake
1 garlic clove, finely chopped

TIP: Don't just stop at cucumbers, this miso mix is a great pickling bed for carrots, cauliflower and daikon too.

Pickled cucumber – part of *tsukemono* miso-pickled vegetables – is a common rice topping and condiment in Japan. Tangy and savoury, the vegetables cease to taste as they did, but become woodier and crunchier, with a snap between your teeth. Smaller cucumbers with less water content work better.

This pickle starts to take shape after two days, but I recommend leaving it for up to five days for a stronger flavour.

Cut the cucumbers in half lengthways and scoop out the seeds with a teaspoon. Lay them curved sides up in a plastic box that will fit the cucumbers in 2 layers.

In a separate bowl, mix both the misos, the sake and garlic together, then spread the mixture on the cucumber, making sure each piece is completely covered from all angles. Cover with a lid and leave in the refrigerator for 2–5 days, to taste. The flavours will become stronger the longer you leave it.

When ready to eat, wash off all the miso under running water, then wipe clean with kitchen paper (paper towels) before slicing and serving.

Serve cold with roasted nuts, on top of cooked rice and noodles, or simply – as I often do – with a plate of cheese and a glass of wine.

In this chapter, we'll move beyond recreating classic Japanese miso dishes and learn how to unlock the powers of miso in your own way, with ingredients that you already have in your kitchen.

With this approach, I intend to allow you to spread your wings: you won't simply be following exacting recipes, but deepening your understanding of how to master miso.

Think of miso as one end of a playground seesaw (teeter). Things get much more interesting when there is a counterbalance, bringing movement and rhythm to a dish. Miso on its own is savoury, deep and complex, but, once you introduce a contrasting flavour, your tastebuds get seriously excited.

By the end of this chapter, you will graduate from knowing *what* to cook with miso to *how* to cook with miso. Understanding how flavours work in unison with miso is key to elevating its usage in your cooking.

Overleaf are the flavour partners that make miso really sing.

If you have a jar of miso at home and you also have some honey, lemon, root ginger or butter, you already have plenty to make a host of exciting dishes. These kitchen staples unite with miso to bring dynamic flavour combinations that will liven up your cooking quickly, using only a few ingredients.

This way of thinking about miso will provide you with a much more intuitive appreciation for how flavour pairing really works. You can read more about how this is underpinned by Japanese principles, as part of Sa-Shi-Su-Se-So, on page 38.

Over time, you will be able to cook with miso without using a recipe at all, knowing that the flavour partners are there to bring balance and roundness to your dish.

This chapter will showcase the best flavour partners, the basis of so many wonderful recipes that I love to cook.

THE FLAVOUR PARTNERS

MISO
+
SWEETNESS

Think maple syrup, sugar, honey.

MISO
+
ACIDITY

Think juices from lemons, limes and oranges, plus other acidic liquids such as wine, fruit and rice vinegars.

MISO
+
FAT

Think creams, milks, cheeses and their dairy-free alternatives.

MISO
+
SPICE

Think chilli (chile), ginger and other seed spices, such as mustard and peppercorns.

ALL-PURPOSE MISO GLAZE OR MARINADE FOR MEAT, FISH OR TOFU

SERVES 2, MAKES ABOUT 100 ML/3½ FL OZ

- 2 tbsp white miso
- ½ tsp soy sauce
- 1 tsp caster (superfine) sugar
- 1½ tbsp water
- 1 tbsp rice vinegar, or apple cider vinegar
- 2½ tsp olive oil
- ½ tbsp toasted sesame oil
- sea salt and freshly ground black pepper

When I am in a rush and just need a quick miso sauce, this is my Everything Miso sauce that works on almost any meats, fish or tofu. It is perfectly balanced, with sweet and acidic notes cutting through the miso, and illustrates that you can add more than one contrasting flavour at a time.

Simply mix together the ingredients in a small bowl and brush on your protein before roasting, grilling (broiling) or frying.

MISO + SWEETNESS

Bringing together sweet and savoury in the same mouthful might be difficult to imagine, but this partnership of flavours is in fact the basis of many of the world's most popular sauces. Think ketchup, teriyaki and barbecue sauces, which surprise and delight our tastebuds time and again.

The recipes in this chapter show you how easy it is to balance miso with a touch of sweetness and create an interesting dish of opposites. With a drizzle of honey or maple syrup, a dash of mirin, a chopped apple or simply a spoonful of sugar, you can transform your flavour-rich miso into something sticky, lively and interesting in minutes.

MISO HONEY CHICKEN WINGS

SERVES 4 AS A STARTER (APPETIZER)

2 tbsp olive oil
1 tbsp sake
12 chicken wings
85 g/3 oz red miso
2 tbsp runny honey
1 tbsp mirin
1 tsp peeled and finely grated root ginger
1 garlic clove, finely grated

A popular cheeky snack in Japan, whether from the hot-hold in your local Family Mart, or carefully grilled (broiled) and served with beers at an *izakaya*. Many a late night in Japan will see me and my friends unable to resist one more pitstop for a snack. This recipe is inspired by those warm nights when we didn't want to go to bed, and the promise of some deeply seasoned chicken wings gave us the excuse to hang out a little longer. Cook these in the oven or on the barbecue (grill) and enjoy with a crunchy salad and a cold beer.

You'll notice that this recipe is an exception to the rules of how to cook with miso (see page 32). You cannot add the miso at the end of cooking, or heat it only gently, when you are grilling chicken wings: you just have to go for it!

Rub the olive oil and sake into the chicken wings in a bowl, cover and leave for at least 30 minutes, or even refrigerate overnight.

Meanwhile, in a bowl, stir together the miso, honey and mirin until smooth, then add the ginger and garlic. Add the chicken to the miso marinade and, using your hands, rub the marinade into the chicken. Cover and leave in the refrigerator for at least 2 hours, or overnight.

When you're ready to cook, preheat the oven to 160°C fan/180°C/350°F/gas mark 4.

Take the chicken out of the marinade, keeping enough marinade on to bring flavour but not so much that it could burn. If cooking on a barbecue (grill), thread the wings on to skewers, so they are easier to turn.

Roast for 15 minutes, before transferring to a hot preheated grill (broiler). Grill for 4–6 minutes on each side until cooked through and the skin is dark and caramelized in spots.

GRILLED GREEN BEAN SALAD WITH SWEET WALNUT MISO DRESSING

SERVES 4–6 AS A SIDE DISH

---

50 g/1¾ oz walnut halves
2 tbsp white miso
2 tbsp mirin
2 tsp caster (superfine) sugar
1 tsp soy sauce
250 g/9 oz green beans, trimmed
a little olive oil
sea salt

This is one of my most repeated make-ahead dishes when I have guests. It acts as a great starter (appetizer), as well as a side dish to fish or meat. The nutty topping sits quite happily on the green beans at room temperature for many hours before serving.

Miso loves nuts and anything a little fatty; here, walnuts cut through the strong notes in the miso to create a satisfying deeply roasted flavour. You can also enjoy this dressing on Tenderstem broccoli (broccolini), asparagus and artichokes.

Preheat the oven to 140°C fan/160°C/325°F/gas mark 3.

Toast the walnuts on a baking tray in the oven for 5 minutes until golden, taking care not to burn them. Remove and leave to cool.

Mix the miso with the mirin, sugar and soy sauce in a small bowl.

Preheat the grill (broiler) to medium. Cook the green beans in a saucepan of salted boiling water for 3 minutes until al dente, then brush with olive oil and grill for 1 minute until slightly charred. You can also fry them in a frying pan (skillet), if you prefer.

Once the walnuts are cold, pulse-blend in a food processor for 20 seconds; you still want some crumbly texture, so be careful they do not become too fine. Mix with the miso sauce, adding a little water to loosen the mixture.

When you are ready to serve, toss the green beans and walnut miso in a mixing bowl until the beans are well coated in the savoury nutty dressing.

ROAST DUCK, CUCUMBER AND SWEET DARK MISO SAUCE

SERVES 4

- 4 tbsp *hatcho* (pure soya bean) miso
- 2 tsp peeled and finely grated root ginger
- 240 ml/9 fl oz mirin
- 120 ml/4½ fl oz sake
- 4 tbsp caster (superfine) sugar
- 4 duck breasts
- 2 tbsp olive oil, plus more for the cucumbers
- 1 tbsp sea salt, plus more for the cucumbers
- 2 small cucumbers, each about 20 cm/8 in long

TIP: This sauce will keep for a week to be enjoyed with other grilled meats, fish or vegetables.

TIP: *Hatcho* miso can be dry and lumpy in texture, so whisk the sauce for a few minutes to thin down.

When *hatcho* miso is sweetened, it has a very similar flavour profile to the Chinese hoisin sauce which is often served with duck. That is the inspiration behind this dish.

In a small mixing bowl, blend the miso, ginger, mirin and sake until the miso is smooth and thinned down.

In a small saucepan, heat the miso mixture over a low heat for 5 minutes before adding the sugar. Stir until the sugar has dissolved, then continue to cook for another 40 minutes over a low heat until the mixture has reduced and is thick and glossy. Try to stir every 10 minutes, to make sure the heat is being distributed evenly.

Brush the duck breasts with the 2 tbsp olive oil and sprinkle with the 1 tbsp salt over both sides, rubbing it in.

Meanwhile, peel and slice the cucumber into coins and place on a foil-lined baking tray. Drizzle with olive oil and sprinkle with a pinch of salt. Preheat the oven to 160°C fan/180°C/350°F/gas mark 4.

Heat up a frying pan (skillet) for 2 minutes before placing in the duck breasts, skin side down. Cook for 4–5 minutes until golden and crispy. A lot of fat will seep out, so try to drain it off to keep the skin crisp. Set the duck aside on another foil-lined baking tray, skin side up. Paint the skin with the miso sauce. Turn the duck over and paint the underside, too. Finally, flip the breasts back over and paint another layer of the sauce on the skin.

Place the duck on a shelf near the top of the oven and the cucumber on a shelf towards the bottom and cook for 15–18 minutes. The duck should be cooked through with a small amount of pink in the flesh. Even if there is not much pinkness, don't worry, the miso has coddled the duck, creating a steaming effect, so the meat will be very tender. Remove the duck and cucumber and let rest for 5–10 minutes.

Slice the duck. Paint another layer of the miso sauce on the duck skin, then drizzle more sauce over the cucumber.

BRAISED MISO PORK RIBS WITH STICKY MISO PLUM SAUCE

SERVES 4

For the ribs
800 ml/1 pint 7 fl oz Dashi (see page 40), or chicken stock
2 tbsp white miso
1 cm/½ in root ginger, peeled and julienned
2 spring onions (scallions), finely chopped
8 large pork ribs

For the plum sauce
8 tbsp plum jam (jelly)
70 g/2½ oz red miso
2 tsp peeled and finely grated root ginger
2 tsp mirin

Pork ribs, when the meat just falls off the bones, are my food heaven. The double miso hit here gives great depth of flavour, while the sticky sweet-and-sour plum sauce makes it a jammy treat. Eat, with glee, with your hands, and don't forget the napkins!

If you have a large enough saucepan, you can simmer the whole rack without separating it into individual ribs, then grill them and carve at the table.

These are lovely served with a sharp and creamy slaw (see page 136).

In a saucepan, heat up the dashi or stock to a rolling boil. Take a ladleful and put into a small bowl. Mix with the miso until smooth, then return the mixture to the pan. Add the julienned ginger and the spring onions.

Reduce the heat and add the pork ribs, then simmer for 60–75 minutes until tender, regularly skimming off any impurities in the water. Drain the ribs and set aside to cool.

Preheat the grill (broiler) to high. Put the jam into a small saucepan over a low heat. Add the red miso, grated ginger and mirin and stir until the miso paste is combined and the sauce is smooth.

Pour the sauce over the cooked ribs and, using a pastry brush, ensure that the ribs are well coated. Place under the preheated grill for 2–3 minutes on each side before serving.

BARLEY MISO AND MAPLE ROAST ROOT VEGETABLES

SERVES 4 AS A SIDE DISH

- 3 large carrots, peeled and chopped into large batons
- 2 small sweet potatoes, peeled and chopped into wedges
- 3 large parsnips, peeled and roughly chopped
- 12 Brussels sprouts
- 3 tbsp olive oil
- 70 g/2½ oz barley miso
- 1½ tbsp runny honey
- 2 tsp water

Barley miso not only has deep savoury flavours, but also a fruity note, as well as a nutty aftertaste, which all work particularly well with root vegetables. Starchy veg are begging for a bit of umami: think potatoes, carrots and parsnips. Pumpkins and swedes (rutabagas) love miso, too. Roasting vegetables with miso is a speedy way to add depth of flavour with very little effort.

Do make sure that the miso sauce is basted on to the vegetables only halfway through cooking and not at the start, as miso burns easily.

The maple syrup not only balances the savoury miso flavours, but also encourages some caramelization, which will upgrade your veggies with a golden hue and crunch. Serve these alongside a Sunday roast with gravy, and your guests will be reaching for the trimmings far more than usual. (For more ways to elevate your Sunday roast with miso, head to page 181.)

Preheat the oven to 160°C fan/180°C/350°F/gas mark 4.

Par-cook the vegetables in a saucepan of boiling water for 6–8 minutes, then drain well and tip into a roasting tray, brush with the olive oil and roast for 20 minutes.

Mix together the barley miso, honey and measured water in a small bowl. Brush on to the vegetables and roast for another 15 minutes, until golden and tender. They will be darker and a little caramelized.

PORK CHOPS WITH APPLE MISO CARAMEL

SERVES 2

3 tbsp water
3 tbsp light brown sugar
2 tbsp rice wine vinegar, or apple cider vinegar
1½ tbsp white miso
2 bone-in pork chops
1 tbsp neutral oil, such as vegetable oil
1 large tart apple, such as Granny Smith, peeled, cored and sliced into 5 mm/¼ in thick wedges
sea salt and freshly ground black pepper

Inspired by dishes that feature both sweet and savoury flavours and a glossy sauce – such as teriyaki salmon, Vietnamese caramel pork belly or Filipino adobo – this dish is a real treat for the senses. You have the umami oomph from the miso with the apple sweetness standing up against the fatty meat. Lush!

Miso makes pork taste more like pork, while the chunky apples make this dish a delight to look at. The marinade works well with gamey meats such as duck and venison as well. Make sure you choose a tart cooking apple, to prevent it all becoming too sweet.

First make the sauce by mixing together the measured water, brown sugar, vinegar and miso until the paste is completely smooth.

Pat the pork chops dry, then season with salt and pepper.

Heat a heavy frying pan (skillet) over a medium heat and add the oil. After 1 minute, add the pork chops. Flip after 2 minutes, then repeat until the pork chops are brown on both sides and cooked through; this takes about 10–15 minutes. If the chops have fat along the edges, use tongs to hold the chops on their sides to gild the fatty rind on the pan directly, to cook the fat and render them golden. Transfer the chops to a plate to rest and pour off and discard any fat from the pan.

Add the apple wedges to the pan in a single layer and place over a medium heat for 4 minutes, turning them carefully to cook them on all sides.

Pour in the sweet miso sauce and, once it starts to melt, keep it stirring and thickening for 2 minutes. Take care not to burn it. Turn off the heat, then return the pork chops together with their juices and coat everything in the miso caramel.

Serve the pork chops with a couple of apple wedges and the caramel.

MISO + ACIDITY

With its rich and dense flavour profile, miso loves a touch of acidity for balance at the same time as adding a fresh layer of flavour. Pair miso with a squeeze of lemon or lime juice for a zingy lightness, or orange or mandarin juice for a floral scent to bring out miso's natural sweetness.

This flavour partnership is the perfect base for salad dressings and marinades, especially when they will be used for oily or rich ingredients, such as fish, seafood and fattier meats.

Beyond fresh fruits, consider making use of fermented sources of acidity too, such as rice, fruit or wine vinegars. The job of the acid prevents miso sauces from becoming too heavy and cloying. It also helps to give sauces a silkier texture that coats leaves, fish and meat easily.

The recipes in this chapter will certainly brighten and perk up your mealtimes.

MISO SALAD DRESSINGS

Having a great miso dressing up your sleeve is key to enjoying salads all year around. These take just minutes to make, and store for up to a week in the refrigerator, so I highly recommend making a bigger batch. Here are my three favourite miso salad dressings that cover all your needs: citrus, punchy and creamy. They all follow the Sa-Shi-Su-Se-So (see page 38) formula of addictive flavour combinations.

Choose a light miso for salad dressings, since darker miso flavours risk being too dominant in a light salad. The acidity in each dressing helps to emulsify the miso with the oils neatly.

Simply whisk the ingredients of each together until emulsified. Each makes enough for 3–4 portions of salad.

THE CITRUS ONE

2 tbsp white miso
1 tbsp runny honey, or maple syrup
1 tbsp toasted sesame oil
2 tbsp apple cider vinegar, or rice wine vinegar
finely grated zest of 1 lemon, plus 2 tbsp lemon juice
2 tbsp olive oil

This is especially good with any fish, prawns (shrimp), chicken, tofu, chickpeas, beans, avocado, eggs and sweetcorn. You can also swap the juice and zest of lemon for orange, mandarin or lime.

THE PUNCHY ONE

2 tbsp white miso
2 tsp wholegrain mustard
1 tbsp olive oil
1 tbsp runny honey
2 tbsp apple cider vinegar

Designed for salads that include roast vegetables, stronger protein flavours such as red or gamey meats, or oily fish like sardines and mackerel. This stands up to stronger flavoured leaves such as rocket (arugula) or chicory (endive) too.

THE CREAMY ONE

2 tbsp white miso
120 ml/4 fl oz tahini
2 tbsp maple syrup
1 tbsp apple cider vinegar, or rice vinegar
4 tbsp water

Great with chicken, tuna, tofu, tomatoes, cucumber and seaweed and incredible on soba noodles. When you are making this, don't worry about the tahini tightening up into a cement-like texture: as soon as you add the water, it will release the tahini into a silky sauce again. If you want the dressing to be thinner, simply add another 1 tbsp water to the recipe.

GRILLED MACKEREL WITH MISO ORANGE SAUCE

SERVES 4 AS A STARTER

4 tbsp white miso
1 tbsp mirin
1 heaped tsp finely grated orange zest, plus 2 tbsp orange juice
1 tbsp water
4 mackerel fillets

TIP: Whizz up plain grilled mackerel with the orange miso marinade in a food processor for a zingy miso mackerel pâté to serve on toasts as a canapé.

Orange and miso are a delightful pairing. Here, the citrus cuts through the sweet buttery oils of the mackerel to balance its richness. Serve with bitter leaves and toasted bread for a light lunch. This dressing is also lovely on other oily fish such as tuna and salmon.

Make the marinade by loosening the miso with the mirin in a small bowl, adding the orange zest and juice with the measured water and stirring until smooth.

Coat the mackerel fillets on both sides with the marinade, cover and leave for 20 minutes.

Preheat the grill (broiler) to medium.

Place the mackerel fillets under the grill, skin side up, for 6 minutes, then turn and grill for a further 2 minutes. The miso can catch and burn quite easily, so keep a close eye on it.

Serve with a salad dressed simply in olive oil and lemon juice.

LEMON MISO CHICKEN HOT POT

SERVES 4

For the chicken and marinade
6 skin-on bone-in chicken thighs and 4 chicken drumsticks
2 tbsp sake
1 tbsp toasted sesame oil
50 g/1¾ oz white miso
2 tbsp red miso
1 tbsp finely grated lemon zest, plus 3 tbsp lemon juice (keep the squeezed-out lemon shell)
1 tbsp mirin
1 tsp yuzu juice, or lemon juice
sea salt

For the rest
1 garlic clove, crushed
1 small onion, finely chopped
2 parsnips, peeled and sliced into wedges
2 small carrots, peeled and sliced into wedges
a little olive oil
200 ml/7 fl oz water
2 tbsp chopped parsley leaves

An easy one-pot that is hearty and full of flavour. It tastes like it has been simmering for hours because of the depth of flavour in the broth, when in fact it is a quick weeknight meal you can pull together very speedily.

The lemon and herbs bring freshness to the juicy chicken thighs and cut through the savouriness of the miso. The warm liquor that the chicken simmers in is irresistible poured over warm rice. Nestled on a bed of root vegetables, the chicken steams inside its pot. Serve with some simple Savoy cabbage and mashed potato for a proper winter warmer.

Put the chicken in a medium bowl. Pour the sake and sesame oil over with a pinch of salt. Rub it all over the chicken, then leave for 15 minutes.

In a small mixing bowl, combine all the other ingredients for the marinade until smooth, then pour over the chicken and rub again.

In a heavy-based casserole (Dutch oven), cook the garlic, onion, parsnips and carrots for 5 minutes in the olive oil until golden.

In a frying pan (skillet), sear the chicken pieces for 3–4 minutes so the skin becomes golden brown, charred in places and crispy on each side. Add the chicken to the casserole, sitting it on top of the vegetables.

Keep all the leftover marinade from the bowl the chicken was marinating in and swirl the measured water around in it until the bowl is clean of miso. Add it to the pot. Slice the lemon that has been squeezed in half and throw into the pot with the parsley.

Reduce the heat, cover and cook for 25 minutes.

ROAST WATERMELON SASHIMI WITH MISO

MAKES 200–300 G/7–10½ OZ, ENOUGH FOR 6 POKÉ BOWLS OR 4 SALADS

1 medium watermelon, to yield 700–900 g/1 lb 9 oz–2 lb watermelon flesh, rind and seeds removed
2 tbsp toasted sesame seeds, to serve

For the marinade (for 200 g/ 7 oz roasted watermelon)
1 tsp white miso
1 tbsp toasted sesame oil
1 tbsp light soy sauce
1 tsp balsamic vinegar
1 tsp toasted nori sheets, ground into powder (see the tip below), or sliced as small as possible

TIP: This marinade is for 200 g/ 7 oz of roasted watermelon, so scale it up if you have more.

TIP: Nori sheets from a packet are already toasted, and normally I put them in a spice grinder to make a powder. (You can also buy it in a ready-ground form, aonori; you can get this from Japanese supermarkets.)

This is a bit of wild one: you won't believe what you are eating! I developed it as a special centrepiece for vegans at barbecues (cookouts) and picnics. Vegan offerings can often feel like an afterthought at such events, but this 'tuna' sashimi will be the star of any meal. It is surprisingly easy to make and requires only a few ingredients. I usually try to find a Spanish watermelon, both for its small size and because they tend to have fewer seeds.

Enjoy as a summery poké bowl over rice, with avocado and mango. It's also delicious inside sushi rolls, or simply sliced and added to salads, or on its own as you would eat traditional sashimi.

Preheat the oven to 180°C fan/200°C/400°F/gas mark 6.

First, slice the watermelon flesh into long wedges, roughly 15 x 7.5 x 7.5 cm/6 x 3 x 3 in. Note that these will shrink considerably. Place them in a large non-stick roasting tin (pan), without any oil. Make sure that none of the pieces are touching: use 2 tins if you need more room.

Roast for 60 minutes. The watermelon will shrink and become bright red in colour as the water evaporates. There may be a little charring around the edges, too. Remove from the oven and leave until completely cold.

Place all the marinade ingredients except for the nori in a mixing bowl. Stir together until smooth, taking care not to leave any lumps of miso paste. Transfer to an airtight container large enough to hold the watermelon, too.

Add the cold watermelon to the marinade, coating each piece in the marinade. Sprinkle the nori on top and give it a final mix through. Leave in the refrigerator for at least 3 hours, but preferably overnight.

When ready to serve, place the watermelon 'fillets' on a chopping board and sprinkle evenly with the toasted sesame seeds. With a sharp knife, slice the fillets diagonally to create even pieces of watermelon sashimi.

2

ASPARAGUS AND POACHED EGGS WITH MISO HOLLANDAISE

SERVES 4

For the sauce
150 g/5½ oz sweet white miso
1 tbsp sake
1 tsp rice vinegar
4–6 tbsp water
1 tbsp caster (superfine) sugar
2 egg yolks
50 g/1¾ oz unsalted butter, chopped

To serve
1 bunch of asparagus
4 eggs
drop of white wine vinegar
pinch of smoked paprika
toast

Su-miso is a traditional Japanese sauce made from rice vinegar and miso paste. It can pep up any cooked green vegetable, such as asparagus or green beans. I have adapted the idea here to make what I call a miso hollandaise, as part of a fancy brunch or starter (appetizer). Try this sauce on classic eggs benedict or florentine, for an indulgent brunch.

In a heatproof bowl, thin the miso down with the sake and vinegar until smooth, then pour in the measured water and stir until smooth once more. Add the sugar and mix again. Add the egg yolks and stir well.

Now place the bowl over a saucepan of simmering water set over a low heat (make sure the bowl does not touch the water). Cook slowly, stirring constantly, for 6 minutes, until the sauce is thickened. Add the butter slowly, while whisking, to prevent splitting. If you are not using the sauce at once, place in a bowl of iced water to rapidly cool the mixture, before refrigerating.

Steam the asparagus for 4 minutes until tender.

Poach the eggs one at a time, breaking them into boiling water mixed with the drop of white wine vinegar to help the whites hold together. (See page 82 for detailed instructions about how to make perfect poached eggs.)

Pour the miso hollandaise over the plated-up eggs and asparagus and finish with the pinch of smoked paprika. Serve with a generous pile of toast, to mop up the tasty sauce.

LEMON MISO MACKEREL SCOTCH EGGS

MAKES 2

For the scotch eggs
3 mackerel fillets, with skin on
2 small eggs
handful of fresh chives, finely chopped
finely grated zest of 2 lemons
1 tbsp white miso
1½ tbsp full-fat cream cheese

To coat and fry
100 g/3½ oz plain (all-purpose) flour
vegetable oil, to deep fry
1 egg, lightly beaten
100 g/3½ oz panko crumbs

TIP: For a rounder, more floral result, try using the finely grated zest of 1 orange instead of the lemon zest.

One of my classic starters for Christmas Day, but also great as a weekend lunch. It looks effortful, but in fact you can easily do the work the night before, and unlike its porky counterpart it cooks more quickly too. Mackerel is a great affordable and sustainable fish that has the richness of meat here.

It is best to use fresh mackerel fillets here, rather than smoked mackerel, since they tend to be ready-salted, making the recipe unbalanced with the miso. If this is all you can find, then honey-smoked mackerel will help to balance the umami from the miso.

I won't lie: you need to nail the egg. Concentrate and don't do anything else while you boil them; once they have the perfect consistency, the rest is easy.

These are great with tartare sauce, Miso Banana Ketchup (see page 156) or wholegrain mustard. Serve with bitter leaves, such as rocket (arugula) and chicory (endive) dressed with olive oil and vinegar.

Bring a deep sauté pan of water to the boil, add the mackerel fillets and reduce the heat to a simmer. Gently bubble for 3 minutes. With a fish slice or broad spatula, lift the fish out on to kitchen paper (paper towels) to absorb any excess water. Once the mackerel has cooled down, peel off the skin and discard.

In a small saucepan, bring enough water to cover both eggs to a rapid boil. Add the eggs and boil for strictly 5½ minutes, while you prepare a bowl of iced water. Plunge the eggs into the icy water to arrest the cooking. This keeps them nice and fudgy in the middle. Once the eggs are cold, peel them.

Break up the mackerel into small pieces and place into a bowl. Then, with a spoon, mix in the chives, lemon zest, miso and cream cheese until you have a smooth paste. Split the mixture into 2 even-sized balls.

Continues overleaf

Place the flour on a plate and dust the cold boiled eggs with the flour (this helps them bind to the mackerel mixture).

Take a piece of clingfilm (plastic wrap) about 30 cm/12 in wide and place it on your hand. Add a mackerel ball and flatten it down on your palm into a patty, making sure it is even in thickness. Now carefully place a flour-dusted egg in the middle of the patty, and, with the aid of the clingfilm, wrap the mackerel mix around the egg carefully. You may have to tidy up by hand to ensure the egg is completely and evenly covered by the mackerel mix and wrapped fully by the clingfilm. Repeat with the second egg, then chill both wrapped scotch eggs in the refrigerator for at least 1 hour to firm up.

When you are ready to cook, fill up a pan with at least 7.5 cm/3 in of vegetable oil and heat to 170°C/340°F.

Put the lightly beaten egg and the panko crumbs in 2 shallow dishes. Make sure the plate of flour is close to hand, too.

Unwrap the scotch eggs and, one at a time, dip them fully in the egg, then coat in the plain flour, then dip once more into the egg and, finally, into the panko crumbs. Make sure every part is covered in the crumbs.

Fry the scotch eggs one at a time for 2 minutes or until golden. Remember the filling is already cooked through, so this is simply to create the crunchy crust. Remove from the oil with a slotted spoon to a plate lined with kitchen paper, to blot excess oil.

With a sharp knife, slice the scotch eggs in half lengthways and serve.

MISO AND LIME GLAZED SALMON

SERVES 4

100 g/3½ oz white miso
20 ml/¾ fl oz mirin
finely grated zest of 2 limes, plus 1 tbsp lime juice
1½ tsp toasted sesame oil
25 g/1 oz caster (superfine) sugar
2 tsp rice vinegar
2 tsp water
a little flavourless oil
500–600 g/1 lb 2 oz–1 lb 5 oz salmon fillet, or 4 individual fillets, skin on

To serve
2 tbsp finely sliced spring onions (scallions)
1 tsp toasted sesame seeds

This doubles up as my all-purpose glaze for any fish. The recipe here is what I make when I need to feed a crowd quickly and want to look like I have made an effort. I have wheeled this out on Christmas Day, New Year's Eve, birthdays and barbecues (cookouts). It takes a few minutes to mix the glaze, but once it has been spread on top of the salmon, your work is done. No marinating time is needed: in the oven it goes, then you just steam some rice and greens to go with it. The miso brings out the deep, meaty flavours of the fish while the lime keeps it light and fresh.

The clever part of this dish is the way the protein in the miso provides a cosy coating for the salmon, forcing it to steam-cook without losing its moisture. This keeps the fish impossibly moist and with a slight feathery texture that is oily and succulent. To ensure this happy result happens for you, really make sure the salmon is fully covered in the miso sauce, so that there are no gaps where any direct heat can get in and dry it out. But, at the same time, make sure there is no more than 3 mm/⅛ in of marinade on top of the salmon, otherwise you could risk having 'toomami' (see page 33).

If you don't have lime, you can also swap it with lemon, yuzu, orange or even mandarin juice and zest.

To make the marinade, thin down the miso with the mirin, lime juice, sesame oil, sugar, rice vinegar and measured water in a small bowl and stir until smooth and combined. Next, add the lime zest and stir again.

Oil a baking tray and line it with baking paper (parchment paper). Lay the salmon on the tray skin side down and spread the marinade on top in an even layer. Make sure you cover the sides of the salmon too. Leave for a maximum of 30 minutes before roasting: miso can draw the water out of salmon and dry it out if you leave it too long.

When ready to cook, preheat the oven to 180°C fan/200°C/400°F/gas mark 6. Bake for 20–23 minutes, until the marinade is golden and bubbling on top.

Sprinkle with spring onions and sesame seeds before serving.

MISO + FAT

I have never been shy about adding butter or cream to dishes; they bring instant decadence. But since I discovered that all buttery and creamy dishes were even better with a touch of white miso, a block of miso butter now happily sits in the refrigerator ready to elevate my dishes at all times.

Miso brings a depth to dairy-based recipes. This depth is sometimes hard to achieve without adding more rich ingredients, such as cheese or bacon, which can mean dishes can become overwhelmingly heavy when actually you were trying to reach for a more profound note. Other umami-rich ingredients that can help are porcini, truffle or pancetta, but if you are looking for something a little more subtle, economical and humble – and vegetarian, to boot – look no further than miso. It brings saltiness, umami depth, a little sweetness and less fat (and cost!) than the alternatives.

The dishes in this chapter take creamy dishes to the next level: think risottos, pastas, chowders and even a slaw. I also share my simple miso butter recipe, which should be in every cook's refrigerator.

MISO BUTTER 5 WAYS

Miso butter has long held a special spot in my already-crammed refrigerator. For me, it is an essential and convenient base for bringing flavour to wilted spinach, steamed peas, a bowl of spaghetti, a slice of sourdough bread, a risotto, a baked potato, or simply a slice melting over grilled (broiled) fish or seared steak. I love to sizzle fresh seafood in a pan with hot melted miso butter too. In fact, it is hard to come up with many dishes that cannot be enhanced by this golden bar of deliciousness. As well as my classic basic recipe, I've given five more ways in which you can use miso butter to make your world a better place.

Once you are happy with your batch of butter, it is best to refrigerate it in a log shape, then slice that into coins and freeze those. This makes dispensing miso butter into your every dish even quicker and simpler!

BASIC MISO BUTTER

MAKES 1 LOG

150 g/5½ oz white miso
200 g/7 oz unsalted butter, at room temperature

This is my classic miso butter recipe, which you can adapt as you please.

Simply beat together the miso with the unsalted super-soft butter in a bowl until smooth and completely combined. It is very important that the butter is super-soft; I like to leave it out overnight so that blending it with miso is effortless.

GRILLED SWEETCORN WITH MISO CHIVE BUTTER

MAKES 1 LOG

150 g/5½ oz white miso
200 g/7 oz unsalted butter, at room temperature
30 g/1 oz fresh chives, finely chopped
4 sweetcorn cobs (ears)
2 tsp Japanese 7-spice powder, or chilli (chile) powder (optional)

TIP: This miso chive butter is really addictive simply spread on toast, or melted as a sauce for seafood, especially scallops or prawns (shrimp). Try it with different fresh herbs such as tarragon and parsley instead of chives, too.

Once you have tried this, you will not want to eat sweetcorn in any other way. Here, miso butter is brushed on to cooked sweetcorn, to glaze and char, creating a smoky and caramelized flavour that brings out the natural sweetness of the corn. The creamy salty flavours are offset by a deep tang, similar to that of a béarnaise sauce, so try this butter on top of steak too. This is a must for all your future barbecues (cookouts).

Put the miso in a bowl and, with a spatula, beat it for 1 minute until it is softer and more pliable, then add the softened butter and beat again for a further minute until fully combined. Sprinkle the chives over and fold in carefully.

Lay out a large piece of clingfilm (plastic wrap) or baking paper (parchment paper) and scrape the butter on to it, then form it into a sausage shape. Gather the ends of the wrap and roll it into a log shape with flat ends.

Place in the refrigerator to chill for at least 2 hours. It will keep here for up to 3 weeks, or wrap it well again and freeze for up to 3 months.

When ready to cook, preheat the oven to 160°C fan/180°C/350°F/gas mark 4, or fire up the barbecue (grill).

Steam the sweetcorn for 5–7 minutes until tender, then brush on the miso butter and put it into the oven or on to the barbecue for a further 5–6 minutes to brown slightly. (If you are cooking on a barbecue, keep turning every 2 minutes to char on all sides.) Sprinkle with a pinch of Japanese 7-spice powder or chilli powder, if you like, then serve.

MISO COCONUT BUTTER BREAKFAST SPREAD

MAKES 1 LOG

150 g/5½ oz white miso
200 g/7 oz coconut butter
2 tsp runny honey, or maple syrup, or to taste

If you are looking for a vegan alternative to miso butter for breakfast, then this is a creamy and sweet pairing and reminds me of the Malaysian kaya paste made from coconut milk and pandan leaves. This is fantastic if you like honey and peanut butter on toast! It has the savoury qualities of a peanut butter but with the sweetness of a French pastry. Great on sweet brioche breads or savoury sourdough. Enjoy with a hot black coffee.

Place the miso paste and coconut butter in a large mixing bowl and, with a wooden spoon, beat the mixture until smooth. This should take about 5 minutes. Gradually drizzle on the honey or maple syrup, until it is sweet enough to your taste.

Lay out a large piece of clingfilm (plastic wrap) in a 50 cm/20 in square. Pour the mixture on to the clingfilm, wrap securely into a log shape and refrigerate for at least 2 hours to firm up. It will keep for up to 3 weeks, or wrap it well again and freeze for up to 3 months.

MISO BUTTER MUSHROOMS WITH BLACK PEPPER

SERVES 4

200 g/7 oz wild mushrooms, roughly chopped if large (see recipe introduction)
50 g/1¾ oz white miso
50 g/1¾ oz unsalted butter, softened
2 tbsp water
2 tbsp olive oil
½ tsp freshly ground black pepper
squeeze of lemon juice

I love mushrooms, and the wilder and more gnarly the better. Go for a mix of textures; juicy oyster mushrooms, meaty shiitake and squeaky chestnut (cremini) mushrooms all help make this dish more interesting.

As the sauce is quite rich, serve it with lean meats, simple greens such as spinach or broccoli and some steamed rice to soak up all that buttery sauce. The generous amount of black pepper adds a warming spice.

Serve these as they are, or on toast, with whipped tofu or ricotta as a base, with a couple of eggs for brunch. You can stir these mushrooms into pasta for a quick dinner too.

Clean the mushrooms to remove any grit.

In a small mixing bowl, blend the miso and butter with the measured water until it forms a smooth paste.

Heat the olive oil in a frying pan (skillet) over a high heat for 1 minute. Add the mushrooms and stir-fry for 2 minutes until they start to soften and take on some colour.

Reduce the heat to low and pour over the miso butter sauce, stirring to ensure the mushrooms are evenly covered. Continue cooking for another 3 minutes while the mushrooms absorb the miso.

Finish with the generous amount of freshly ground black pepper and the lemon juice before serving.

MISO BROWN BUTTER AND CAPER SKATE WINGS

SERVES 2

2 skate wings
25 g/1 oz unsalted butter
1 tbsp olive oil
50 g/1¾ oz Basic Miso Butter (see page 126)
1½ tbsp capers, finely chopped
2 tbsp finely chopped fresh chives
juice of 1 lemon
sea salt and freshly ground black pepper

Skate wings are one of my favourite fish to eat: the flesh is feathery, sweet and hard to overcook, a dinner party dish that always impresses. This miso-brown butter combo is inspired by the way I brown butter for my Miso Brown Butter Banana Bread (see page 200). The brown butter gives nutty tones to the sauce, while the miso strikes a bold note against the sweet creamy fish. The sweet, sharp capers are little gems to surprise the palate. The sauce can be used with any white fish, especially halibut, bass, hake or haddock.

Preheat the oven to 110°C fan/130°C/260°F/gas mark ¾.

Rinse and pat dry the skate wings and season with salt and pepper on both sides.

Melt the unsalted butter and the olive oil in a wide frying pan (skillet). Once the butter is sizzling, lay the skate wings fleshier side down and fry for 5 minutes until the flesh is opaque, before flipping to cook for 3 minutes on the other side. If your pan is not large enough, then cook these one at a time.

Transfer the skate wings to the oven to keep warm.

In a small saucepan, heat up the miso butter until the butter and miso separates and a golden nutty aroma is detected. Remove from the heat and add the capers and chives. Keep whisking the melted butter so that the miso, capers and chives are dispersed through the melted butter.

When ready to serve, squeeze the lemon juice over the skate wings, then plate them up and pour the miso caper butter on top of the fish. Serve with simple greens and potatoes, or rice, to keep the skate wings the main focus of the plate.

CREAMY MISO BUTTER MASHED POTATOES

SERVES 4–6

2 kg/4 lb 8 oz potatoes, such as Maris Piper, Rooster, Yukon Gold or King Edward
250 g/9 oz unsalted butter
200 g/7 oz white miso
120 ml/4 fl oz double (heavy) cream
1 tbsp extra virgin olive oil
1 tbsp finely chopped fresh chives (optional)
sea salt and freshly ground black pepper

TIP: Adding chopped fresh herbs to your miso butter adds a freshness and a further level of flavour. Chives work particularly well, bringing a cheese-and-onion vibe, parsley adds grassy notes and tarragon aniseed and nutty flavours. Adding the finely grated zest of a small lemon will bring out the herby flavours even further. Avoid more pungent herbs, such as coriander (cilantro), rosemary or thyme, as these flavours will fight with the miso and nobody likes a fight!

Upgrade this staple side dish with the savoury notes from miso.

Peel and quarter the potatoes, then place in a large saucepan and pour in water to cover by at least 2.5 cm/1 in.

Season the water generously with salt. Bring the water to the boil over a medium heat and then reduce the heat to a simmer, cooking until the potatoes are very tender and break apart easily, around 20 minutes.

Drain the potatoes and let them sit in the hot dry pan for 5 minutes to dry out.

To make the miso butter, whip the unsalted butter with the miso until smooth. Set aside.

In a small saucepan, bring the cream to a simmer, then remove from the heat.

Put half the miso butter in the pan with the potatoes. Using a potato masher or ricer, smash the potatoes for a few minutes. Add the warm cream, then mash again until smooth. Season with salt and pepper and the olive oil before serving in a large shallow bowl, sprinkling with chives, if you like, and adding a scoop of the remaining miso butter to melt on top as a final flourish.

CREAMY TAHINI MISO SLAW

SERVES 4–6 AS A SIDE DISH

- 250 g/9 oz white cabbage, shredded into long strips
- 150 g/5½ oz red cabbage, shredded into long strips
- 150 g/5½ oz carrot, julienned into 5 cm/2 in strands
- 1 eating apple, grated
- 3 tbsp white miso
- juice of 1 lemon
- 1 tsp peeled and finely grated root ginger
- 1 tsp caster (superfine) sugar
- 3 tbsp tahini
- 2 tbsp natural yogurt
- 1 tbsp olive oil
- 2 spring onions (scallions), finely chopped

This coleslaw uses tahini and yogurt instead of mayonnaise and tastes lighter and more savoury than traditional slaws. It is great with grilled (broiled) meats and fish and, of course, at a barbecue (cookout) or picnic.

The key to getting the dish right is cutting the vegetables as thinly as possible to give them a chance to properly absorb the dressing, as well as to let the flavours sit together for a couple of hours, even overnight, before serving.

Mix both types of cabbage, the carrot and apple in a large bowl and toss together with your hands.

In a small bowl, mix the miso with the lemon juice and stir until smooth. Add the ginger, sugar and tahini and mix again. Finally stir in the yogurt and olive oil and the spring onions.

Pour the dressing over the vegetables and mix thoroughly.

Leave to rest for at least 20 minutes before serving. This keeps for 2 days, covered, in the refrigerator. Stir it before serving.

mixer

BUTTERY MISO MUSHROOM RISOTTO

SERVES 2

- 1½ tbsp white miso, plus 1 tbsp for the broth
- 2 tbsp unsalted butter, at room temperature
- 5 g/1/8 oz dried porcini
- 100 ml/3½ fl oz boiling water
- 3 tbsp extra virgin olive oil
- 400 g/14 oz mixed mushrooms; chestnut (cremini), button and king oyster mushrooms work well
- 1 tsp chopped fresh thyme leaves
- 3 garlic cloves, minced or finely grated
- 1 leek, finely chopped
- 200 g/7 oz arborio rice
- 80 ml/3 fl oz dry white wine
- 20 g/¾ oz Parmesan cheese, or vegetarian Parmesan-style cheese, plus more to serve (optional)
- 2 tbsp finely chopped fresh parsley leaves
- sea salt and freshly ground black pepper

The miso-and-mushroom combo has become popular in recent years. Miso mushroom pastas, miso mushroom pies, miso mushroom pizzas, miso mushroom gravy… the list goes on. It is no wonder this winning formula gets so much airtime: the umami in the miso boosts the umami in the mushrooms and this multiplying effect is seriously addictive, bringing a meatiness to mushrooms that is super-satisfying.

In my risotto, the flavours subtly weave through the sweetness of the rice grains. This is a super-tasty vegetarian dish that can easily be made vegan by swapping out the butter and cheese for suitable substitutes. In fact, miso can bring a cheesy flavour to vegan dishes, naturally.

There are a couple of stages to make this risotto perfect, and patience is one of the key ingredients. If you follow my steps carefully, I promise you the best mushroom risotto you have ever eaten. The key to nailing the dish is to slowly cook the mushrooms, to really concentrate their flavour, before adding miso butter. The leek and mushroom pairing is always a winner, bringing a grassy sweetness to the dish.

For this risotto, a miso broth is used to infuse even more flavour into the grains, in place of stock. Finish with a drizzle of olive oil or truffle oil, or a grating of Parmesan (or vegan substitute), for that final hit of umami.

First make the miso butter by whipping together the 1½ tbsp miso and the butter, then set aside. Place the remaining 1 tbsp miso in a bowl and gradually pour in 400 ml/14 fl oz hot water, stirring all the time, to make a broth.

Put the porcini in a small bowl with the measured boiling water and leave for 20 minutes, then drain.

In a large frying pan (skillet), heat 1 tbsp of the olive oil and cook the mixed mushrooms and porcini over a medium-high heat. Make sure you cook the mushrooms in a single layer; do not overcrowd the pan or they will sweat. The key is to get them to a dark brown colour without burning them. Cook for 8–10 minutes, stirring only occasionally. If you need to do it in 2 batches, please do! It is worth the effort.

Reduce the heat to low and add the chopped thyme and half the garlic to the mushrooms. Season with ½ tsp of salt and stir frequently for 2–3 minutes. Stir in the creamed miso butter and cook for 2 minutes, season with a pinch of salt and pepper, then set aside.

In a heavy-based pan, warm up the remaining 2 tbsp olive oil. Once hot, add the leek and remaining garlic. Cook for 2–3 minutes, until just softened. Add the rice and stir quickly so that all the grains are well coated in the oil. Keep the grains moving in the pan for 60–90 seconds, the rice will start to smell a little bit toasty and golden.

Pour in the wine and stir quickly to scrape up any bits that have stuck to the bottom of the pot. Continue cooking for 3–4 minutes until the boozy note starts to disappear.

Add 100 ml/3½ fl oz of the miso broth and stir occasionally. Once the rice has absorbed the liquid, add the same amount of broth again and continue this process until all the liquid is used up, stirring every 30 seconds. Only add more broth when the previous amount of liquid has been absorbed by the grains. The rice should be firm and creamy, not soft or mushy.

Add the cooked mushrooms and stir them through, then remove from the heat and stir in the cheese, if using. Taste for seasoning, adding salt and pepper if required. Scatter with the parsley and serve immediately with more cheese and a drizzle of oil, if you like.

MISO SEAFOOD BAKED DORIA

SERVES 4

½ tbsp unsalted butter
1 small head of broccoli
finely grated Parmesan or Gruyère cheese, for the top
1 tbsp panko crumbs (optional)

For the rice
1 garlic clove, minced or finely grated
½ onion, finely chopped
1½ tbsp olive oil
1½ tbsp unsalted butter
4 button mushrooms, or chestnut (cremini) mushrooms, finely sliced
2 tsp finely chopped fresh parsley leaves, plus extra to serve
600 g/1 lb 5 oz cooked and cooled Japanese short-grain rice (300 g/10½ oz uncooked rice)
sea salt and freshly ground black pepper

Doria is a Japanese baked rice gratin topped with béchamel and cheese; I see it as Japan's mac and cheese, or lasagne: rich gooey sauce on a bed of carbs. I hunt down doria at affordable chain restaurants in Japan, where you order from a screen and it arrives canteen-style on a tray. It's just what you want on a cool autumn day, plus it reminds me of a Hong Kong Macau-Portuguese seafood baked rice dish, which brings back childhood memories. I have adapted this recipe to suit my taste, as authentic Japanese doria sauce is usually a bit too sweet for my liking. The miso here adds more savouriness and depth to the creamy béchamel.

This could easily slide on to your weekly repertoire as a weeknight dinner, using leftover rice as a base. You can use any mix of seafood you want, I've just included those I had in my kitchen. Traditionally, doria is baked and served in individual bowls, but you could make a one-pan bake for sharing, too. All it needs on the side is a fresh green salad, or steamed greens.

Rub 4 ovenproof dishes, or 1 large ovenproof dish to share, with the butter.

Trim the broccoli into florets. Bring a saucepan of salted water to the boil. Cook the broccoli for 90 seconds, then drain and plunge into cold water, to stop the cooking.

Next, prepare the rice base. Cook the garlic and onion in the olive oil in a sauté pan over a medium heat. Add the butter, mushrooms and parsley and season with salt and pepper. When the mushrooms are softened and golden brown, stir in the cooked rice, making sure it is coated in all the flavours.

Split the rice between the prepared dishes or large dish and leave to cool.

Meanwhile, cook the seafood. Warm up the olive oil in a frying pan – make sure it has a lid if you are using shellfish – then add the garlic. Add all your seafood and stir to coat in the garlicky oil, then pour in the white wine, cover if you have shellfish in the pan, and cook for a further 2 minutes until the seafood is cooked through. Remove any

For the seafood
2 tbsp olive oil
2 garlic cloves, minced
10 clams or mussels
12 queen scallops
8 calamari rings
120 ml/4 fl oz white wine

For the béchamel
4 tbsp unsalted butter
4 tbsp plain (all-purpose) flour
480 ml/17 fl oz full-fat milk
1½ tsp white miso
¼ tsp paprika

---

shellfish that have not opened, then remove the rest with a slotted spoon and place on a plate, covered with foil to keep them warm. Simmer the seafood sauce remaining in the pan until thickened, then take off the heat.

Now for the béchamel. In a pan, melt the butter, then add the flour. It will form a paste: keep it moving in the pan to ensure the flour is cooked. Slowly add the milk, stirring all the time, to create a thin sauce. Take 2 tbsp of the sauce out, place into a small bowl and mix in the miso until you have a smooth paste, then pour this back into the béchamel sauce in the pan to combine. Season with pepper and the paprika.

Keep the béchamel over a low heat and reduce it until thick, then add the reserved seafood sauce. Once you can draw a line at the bottom of the pan using your spatula, the sauce is thick enough.

Preheat your grill (broiler) to its hottest setting.

Now stir the seafood and broccoli into the sauce. Layer this on the rice, making sure each person has a good mix of vegetables and seafood.

Top with Parmesan or Gruyère, panko if using, and a sprinkle of parsley, then grill for 2–3 minutes until the cheese has melted and the crumbs are golden.

Pictured overleaf

MISO UDON CARBONARA WITH DUCK EGG

SERVES 3

---

3 bacon rashers (slices), chopped into 1 cm/½ in chunks
1 tbsp olive oil
2 garlic cloves, minced or finely grated
140 ml/4½ fl oz full-fat milk
100 g/3½ oz finely grated Parmesan cheese, plus more to serve
¼ tsp freshly ground black pepper, plus more to serve
1 heaped tbsp white miso
2 frozen udon noodle nests (or see recipe introduction)
3 duck egg yolks (or see recipe introduction)

Call me a *gaishin* (Japanese for 'foreigner'), but I don't just adore Japan for its native cuisine, I also secretly love the country for its Italian dishes. I have never been a purist, and the Japanese take on Italian dishes is charming. The tomato sauces are a little sweeter, the creamy sauces have a touch of umami and the pasta has a bounce that could only come from the touch of noodle masters.

This dish exemplifies what I love about that fusion of cuisines. The udon is chewy rather than al dente; the sauce is creamy, but with a depth that stops it from getting too rich. And the duck egg adds an unusual hit of gameyness such as that you might expect from a ragu. If you can't get duck eggs, you can use regular hen's eggs, but try to make sure you get the type with bright orange yolks.

If you don't have frozen udon, pre-cooked packs work too, but you won't experience the chewy texture.

In a frying pan (skillet) over a medium heat, cook the bacon until the edges become dark and crispy. Remove from the pan and set aside.

In the same pan, warm up the olive oil and cook the garlic over a low heat for 1 minute until golden. Add the milk to the pan, and, once bubbling, add the cheese until it melts, then the black pepper. Whisk in the miso paste carefully so that there are no lumps in the sauce. Take the pan off the heat.

Pop the kettle on and, in a large bowl, soak the frozen udon nests in boiling water for 2 minutes until just softened.

To bring the dish together, put the frying pan back over a low heat to warm up the sauce again. Take the udon out of the water with tongs and add to the sauce, mixing to coat the noodles, then take off the heat. Scatter with the reserved crispy bacon.

Now you can choose how to finish the dish. Either pour the egg yolks over the noodles and mix through in the pan, or serve up the noodles with an egg yolk on top of each serving, for people to mix in themselves, for more dramatic effect. Add a final crack of black pepper and sprinkle of Parmesan, then serve immediately.

MISO CLAM CHOWDER

SERVES 4

400 g/14 oz clams in their shells
750 ml/1¼ pints Dashi (see page 40)
1 tbsp olive oil
1 bacon rasher (slice), finely chopped
1 small onion, finely chopped
1 tbsp plain (all-purpose) flour
1 small potato, peeled and cut into 1 cm/½ in squares
2 bay leaves
1 tsp fresh thyme leaves
2 tbsp sweet white miso
1 tbsp white miso
250 ml/9 fl oz soya milk
2 tbsp chopped fresh chives
sea salt

TIP: Never boil soya milk, as it curdles! It's best to keep the heat off, or just on a low simmer, when adding soya milk to hot liquids.

During one of my trips to Japan, we stayed in a traditional hot spring hotel in Suwa, near Nagano. For breakfast, we were served miso soup every day with fresh clams from the lake the hotel overlooked. I looked forward to it every morning. I love their sweet, almost metallic flavour in this soup.

Back home, I came up with a twist on the classic clam chowder using white miso and soya milk as a base, with bacon bits for extra umami.

First prepare the clams: put them in a colander, then place it in a large bowl of salted cold water. Let them stand for 90 minutes to get rid of any sand. Then give them a good rub and rinse them under cold running water.

Put the dashi and clams in a large saucepan, then bring to the boil over a medium heat. If there is foam, skim it off, then reduce the heat to low and cook for 3–4 minutes until the clams open. Throw away any unopened shells. Strain the clams in a colander over a bowl, reserving the liquid, then strain the liquid through a fine sieve (strainer).

In another large saucepan, heat the olive oil, add the bacon and cook until crispy, then add the onion for another 5 minutes until soft and translucent. Stir in the flour to create a thickened paste, before gradually pouring in the reserved liquid from the clams, stirring all the time. Finally, add the potato, bay leaves and thyme and return the soup to a rolling boil.

Reduce the heat to a simmer. Place both types of miso in a ladle or sieve (strainer). Dip it into the soup so the dashi seeps in, but the miso does not escape into the pot. Slowly loosen up the miso with a spoon inside the ladle or sieve; as the dashi mixes with it, the paste will slowly melt into the dashi.

Return the clams to the soup and bring the mixture to a very gentle simmer again before gradually stirring in the soya milk, then turn off the heat. Take out the bay leaves and serve immediately, sprinkled with the chives.

MISO + SPICE

While spice is not a common ingredient in Japanese dishes, miso is a great partner for certain spices, namely chilli (chile), pepper and ginger. These flavours bring some exciting top notes to dishes, adding new dimensions to humble vegetables, or depth to meatier dishes.

One word of warning: miso does not combine so well with more subtle aromatic spices such as cardamom, coriander seeds, cumin, and garam masala-based curries and sauces. This is because miso has the ability to dull these aromatics and dominate a dish with its umami, so try to avoid partnering miso with those. Stick to chilli, ginger and all kinds of peppercorns and you will have some seriously powerful flavour combinations that will leave your tastebuds singing.

WHOLE ROASTED SPICY LIME CAULIFLOWER

SERVES 4 AS A MAIN DISH, OR 6 AS A SIDE DISH

---

1 head of cauliflower, about 700 g/1 lb 9oz
2 tbsp toasted sesame oil
1 tbsp olive oil
1 tbsp red miso
½ tbsp Chinese chilli-garlic (chile-garlic) sauce
1 tbsp peeled and finely grated root ginger
1 tsp finely grated lime zest, plus 1 tsp lime juice
2 spring onions (scallions), finely sliced
2 tsp toasted white and black sesame seeds

This is a great veggie centrepiece; it looks impressive and cooking the whole head means you create a lovely contrast of smoky dark outer florets with a sweetly steamed inner. Carved up at the dinner table, this feels special. The ginger and lime flavours sing out beautifully. Simply serve with steamed rice and a side salad: let the cauliflower be the centre of attention.

Take care to only add a thin layer of sauce to the cauliflower, as miso can burn quickly. If your cauliflower is quite large, you can add the glaze halfway through the cooking time, to align the timings.

Cut the leaves and stem off the cauliflower so that it sits flat, and wash it gently but well.

In a small bowl, mix together the sesame and olive oils, the miso, chilli-garlic sauce, ginger and lime zest and juice until fully combined. Using your hands, rub the mix over the cauliflower, making sure you get it everywhere, even the base. Leave for 30 minutes.

Preheat the oven to 140°C fan/160°C/325°F/gas mark 3. Put the cauliflower on a baking tray lined with baking paper (parchment paper) and roast for 1 hour. Remove the cauliflower from the oven and sprinkle the spring onions and toasted sesame seeds over.

Slice the cauliflower at the table into wedges, as if cutting a cake.

BLACK PEPPER HATCHO MISO SIRLOIN STEAK

SERVES 4

400 g/14 oz *hatcho* (pure soya bean) miso
120 ml/4 fl oz mirin
120 ml/4 fl oz sake
2 tbsp freshly ground black pepper
2 tbsp peeled and finely grated root ginger
2 garlic cloves, finely grated
2 tsp caster (superfine) sugar
4 sirloin (striploin) steaks, each 150–200 g/5½–7 oz

TIP: With red meats, be careful never to marinate with miso for more than 2 hours, as the meat can dry out, making it tougher.

Hatcho is the deepest-darkest of misos and has Marmite vibes: you either love it or hate it. It has a strong savoury coffee-and-cocoa flavour and the dense colour of dark soy sauce. When I was travelling in the region it is famously made in – the Aichi prefecture – all the local businesses would serve it and you could smell it from outside the restaurants.

Back home, *hatcho* miso works well in small quantities with darker meats, such as beef or game. If you like Chinese black bean sauce, then this *hatcho*-marinated steak will send your tastebuds doolally. The savoury beef flavours are multiplied and rounded off by the smokiness of this miso. It can be a little dry (it has undergone the longest fermentation of all misos) so it will need thinning out first.

Black pepper is key to this dish, as *hatcho* on its own can be heavy and almost dull. A prickle of spice brings *hatcho* to life, so consider pairing this miso with ginger, white pepper and chilli (chile), too.

Thin the miso down by mixing it in a bowl with the mirin and sake to make a soft paste. Add the pepper, ginger, garlic and sugar. As *hatcho* miso is much thicker and more robust in texture than many others, it will take a couple of minutes to make the marinade totally smooth, removing any lumps.

Pour half the mixture into a plastic container or tray in which the steaks can fit without overlapping.

Place 2 layers of kitchen paper (paper towels) over the top of the marinade and flatten down, then place the steaks in a single layer on top of the kitchen paper. Cover with another 2 layers of kitchen paper and spread most of the rest of the miso over it, making a 'sandwich' of steaks protected from the miso marinade by the kitchen paper. Discard any excess marinade. Cover with clingfilm (plastic wrap) and leave for 90 minutes in the refrigerator.

Wipe the beef clean of any miso that has seeped through. By now, the steaks will have taken on the miso flavour without having much direct contact with it. This way of marinating prevents miso catching on the pan and burning.

Heat a large frying pan (skillet), or a griddle (grill) pan and add the steaks. Cook on each side for 2 minutes for medium-rare before turning and cooking for another 2 minutes on the other side (or 2½ minutes on each side for medium). Extend the time if you prefer your steaks to be cooked for longer. Either way, rest the steaks for at least 3 minutes before serving.

Remove the steaks and transfer to warmed plates. Serve with stir-fried or roast vegetables.

MISO HARISSA JACKFRUIT TACOS

SERVES 4

600 g/1 lb 5 oz canned jackfruit, drained
90 g/3¼ oz red miso
200 g/7 oz rose harissa paste (I love Belazu)
1 tbsp extra virgin olive oil, plus more for the trays
30 ml/1 fl oz balsamic glaze, or balsamic vinegar
35 ml/1 fl oz maple syrup

To serve
4 large taco shells or soft tacos
1 ripe avocado, mashed
4 baby tomatoes, halved
4 Baby Gem lettuces
gherkins (pickles) and pickled jalapeños (optional)
grated mild cheese (optional)
squeeze of lime juice

This is a recipe I developed for a TV cookery show, to showcase miso's versatility with flavours from outside Japan.

The pairing of miso and harissa is a killer combo that works particularly well on aubergines (eggplants), sweetcorn and roast meats and fish, as well as this jackfruit, which is also great in pasta and sandwiches. This marinade has it all: sweetness from maple syrup, heat from harissa, umami from miso and acidity from balsamic vinegar. And you have got to try making a bit extra and drizzling it over fried or poached eggs.

Serve with something creamy and fresh for contrast, such as slaw (see page 136), or acidic pickles and cheese on top can bring even more to the party.

Preheat the oven to 160°C fan/180°C/350°F/ gas mark 4.

Rip the jackfruit up with your hands, so that the strands come apart but leave bite-sized chunks. Keep the pieces roughly the same size, for even baking.

To make the marinade, in a large bowl, mix together the miso, harissa, olive oil, balsamic glaze or vinegar and maple syrup until you have a smooth paste. Now add the jackfruit and turn it gently using a wooden spoon, until the pieces are evenly coated but not broken apart any further.

Split the batch of jackfruit across 2 oiled baking trays, leaving plenty of space between the pieces to ensure you get some crispy bits. Reserve the excess marinade. Bake for 30 minutes until golden and slightly charred but not dry, then remove from the oven to cool.

Now you can either fill the tacos yourself or leave it for your guests to make their own. Take a taco shell and layer up the fillings, starting with the mashed avocado as a base. Load up with jackfruit, tomatoes and lettuce. Drizzle over a little of the reserved marinade.

Top with pickles and cheese if you like, though a squeeze of lime juice is compulsory!

MISO BANANA KETCHUP

MAKES 500 ML/18 FL OZ

1 tbsp vegetable oil
1 small red onion, finely chopped
1 tsp peeled and finely grated root ginger
3 garlic cloves, finely chopped
pinch of chilli (chile) flakes
1 tsp ground cinnamon
1 tsp ground allspice
3 tsp Madras curry powder
6 ripe bananas, mashed
3 tbsp dark brown sugar
200 ml/7 fl oz cider vinegar, or rice vinegar
1½ tbsp red miso
sea salt

This sauce exaggerates what makes ketchup… ketchup! I originally made it to accompany my Lemon Miso Mackerel Scotch Eggs (see page 120), but it is actually a great dipping sauce for fried potatoes and seafood, to inject some pzazz into ordinary sandwich fillings, or alongside grilled (broiled) meats such as pork chops or oily fish like salmon or sardines.

We have all the flavours of the Sa-Shi-Su-Se-So principles here (see page 38), the sweetness from banana, the acidity of cider vinegar and the miso for umami: a perfect balance. The peppery notes from the ginger make for a fiery sauce that is then calmed by the fudgy caramel notes from the ripe bananas.

I have also been known to cook salmon fillets in this sauce, as if it were a curry, and serve it with rice: highly recommended!

The recipe makes plenty to enjoy across several meals.

Heat the oil in a frying pan (skillet) and fry the onion over a low heat until caramelized. This will take about 20 minutes.

Next add the ginger, garlic, chilli and cinnamon and stir through until the spices are coated in oil. Add the allspice and curry powder. Keep stirring for 5 minutes until the spices smell aromatic.

Stir in the mashed bananas, sugar, vinegar and miso paste, with a pinch of salt, then let it simmer for 20 minutes until the sauce thickens. If the sauce is too thick, simply add 1 tbsp of water at a time to loosen the texture.

Set aside to cool and then store in a sterilized jar (I usually just wipe a jar with clear alcohol, such as vodka). This will keep in the refrigerator for up to 4 weeks.

SPICY MISO MAYONNAISE

MAKES 300 ML/10 FL OZ

3 egg yolks
1 tsp Dijon mustard
2 tbsp white miso
250 ml/9 fl oz mild olive oil
1 tbsp white wine vinegar
½ tsp lemon juice
paprika

This is a great sauce to have on standby at barbecues (cookouts), or simply for your daily sandwiches and salads. Wonderful on tomatoes, eggs, avocados, seafood and chicken salads. As a dip, it is fantastic served with sweet potato fries, on a prawn (shrimp) cocktail, or mixed with chopped egg for a rich and creamy sandwich filling with zing.

Take care to drizzle the oil into the blender slowly, to prevent splitting. This keeps for a week, covered and in the refrigerator, and is well worth the effort.

In a small bowl, whisk the egg yolks, mustard and white miso until smooth and well combined, then pour into a food processor, or get out a hand-held blender.

While mixing, very slowly add the olive oil, vinegar and lemon juice. Try to drizzle each ingredient in as slowly as you can bear, which should take 3 minutes. The mayonnaise will emulsify and thicken. Add paprika to taste.

This is my favourite chapter. I am going to share with you my greatest discovery in many years of working with magical miso: the utterly transformative quality of adding it at a micro level to your favourite recipes.

In the dishes in other chapters, miso is distinctive, standing out and showing off its charms, its complexity of flavour, funky and varied. So far, we have celebrated miso in classic Japanese recipes and used it to bring a twist to flavour partners such as honey, butter, lemon and chilli.

Now, I am going to show you something completely different – the stealthiest miso trick there is. Miso can seriously transform and improve all your food, in one clever but very simple step. In all my years working in food and developing products, I have learned that attempting to improve existing dishes is far, far more difficult than it is to make something new. It is much easier to use new ingredients in novel combinations, and declare that you have created something exciting, than it is to make a classic dish taste better without fundamentally altering its hallmarks.

Most of us have a few dishes that we are particularly proud of. You might even be requested to make them on occasion; we all have recipes that delight others. Now imagine those favourites, but elevated. Flavours are clearer, cleaner and more punchy: tomato tastes sweeter and more rounded; white sauces have the depth of an aged Parmesan; sourness or bitterness is smoothed away and polished. Flavours taste the way you fantasize they might, at their peak of ripeness and refinement.

If you can believe it, all this is easily achieved with the expert application of miso. This chapter will teach you how adding a secret touch of miso to certain dishes will transform them in your repertoire forever.

THE SECRET WEAPON

THE MAGIC FORMULA

To develop my secret weapon, I started consciously noting which dishes I was adding a spoonful of miso to at the end of cooking, which I had done previously without a second thought. There are certain recipes I always finish with a cheeky addition of miso: it has become instinctive and natural for me.

Dishes that featured tomatoes, cheese, slow-cooked onions or cocoa would all receive a little miso booster at the end. Like adding salt to boiling potatoes, or using starchy pasta-cooking water to make a sauce extra-silky, these little tricks finesse our cooking; once you have tasted the difference they make, you won't skip that step ever again.

At the same time, I looked at the most-repeated home-cooked dishes globally and noted some themes in terms of their base flavours. I was convinced that I could come up with a formula that would work across all cuisines.

With this approach to cooking with miso, we are not adding a new twist and we are certainly not putting in a noticeable miso flavour. Instead, each component of a dish simply now delivers to a higher level.

I have kept the recipes in this chapter fairly light and loose; they are here to illustrate the principles of my formula. But ultimately, once you have learned this trick, you can give many of your favourite dishes a miso makeover.

Miso is not the leader here, but a critical supporting actor. It rounds out a dish and elevates it to heights it has never reached before. You will notice that its subtle role is reflected in how I have named the recipes: each is the god-tier version of a favourite dish.

BOOST YOUR BASE

THE INGREDIENTS THAT MISO SECRETLY BOOSTS

TOMATO

Think bolognese, shakshuka, stews, soups, beans on toast and even a cocktail such as a Bloody Mary. If you are making vegetarian or vegan pasta, miso is the magic wand that brings a richness and depth which is hard to replicate with any other plant-based ingredient. Your spaghetti sauce will taste as though you have been simmering it for hours after just a spoonful of miso: silkier, richer and smoother.

CHEESE AND CREAM

Take nachos with cheese topping, pasta bakes, cheese on toast, risottos, mac and cheese or carbonara. Adding miso makes cheese flavours both more pronounced and as if you have made a recipe from prize-winning 48-month-aged Parmesan, not just from whatever cheese you had in the refrigerator.

SLOW-COOKED ONIONS

Consider pie fillings, soups or the gravy from a Sunday roast. Miso brings out the natural sweetness of onions while adding a meaty depth and body. Again, if you are making vegetarian dishes with an onion base, adding miso will provide the hearty satisfying flavours that are often missing from plant-based sauces.

COCOA

Your brownies, chocolate mousses and cakes can all be elevated with a miso makeover. Miso makes chocolate flavours deeper and even more moreish and balances the sweetness.

TIPS FOR MAKING MISO YOUR SECRET WEAPON

1. HOW MUCH?

Adding only a touch of miso is the key to successfully nailing this approach. You should not be able to actually taste the miso itself in a dish – yes, it should be that stealthy! If you can taste the miso, you have added a little too much! As a guide, I add 1–2 tsp white miso to a can of chopped tomatoes, or to a loaf cake.

Unlike when you put chilli (chile) or a squeeze of lemon juice in a dish – when you taste it and say, 'Ah, there it is!' – this secret ingredient operates at a ninja level. The miso supercharges everything it touches, without being the main character. Adding too much miso in this context is what I call 'toomami': far too much umami. (See page 33.) You can have too much of a good thing! Toomami is an easy mistake to make and I still fall foul of it myself sometimes, but less is more. To avoid toomami, start small, a teaspoon at a time, until you have reached a level that makes the existing flavours deeper and more rounded without any miso flavour coming through.

If you really have overdone it, you will need to even things out by increasing the other ingredients being boosted: perhaps a bit more tomato purée will help, or some extra cheese or – in the case of slow-cooked onions – some water to dilute the miso flavour. Practice makes perfect and you will quickly develop an intuition for how much to add.

2. THIN IT OUT FIRST

Miso can be stubborn; its dense texture does not melt easily into thinner liquids and broths. So simply ladle out a cup of the liquid into a small bowl, into which you mix the miso. The ladle of sauce or broth will thicken and the natural soya lecithin in the miso will emulsify and bind with it, to make it extra-silky in texture.

Once you have an even paste with no lumps, pour it back into the main saucepan and stir back through. This does add a little extra work, but it really saves you time, as well as the effort of whisking out lumpy bits of miso.

3. WHEN TO ADD IT?

Seasoning with miso is best done towards the end of cooking, once the other flavours have already settled down. Miso's flavours alter and become less complex the longer you cook it, so I prefer to add it as late as possible. Baking and desserts are of course the exception and you can find guidance on this in the sweet recipes in this book (see pages 196–215).

4. WHICH TO USE?

There are so many types of miso available, but I recommend a light version (such as a white miso) for tomato and cheese dishes, then for onion-based dishes a blend of light and dark varieties (such as white and red miso). Onions can take a deeper flavour contrast without miso becoming too prominent, but with tomato and cheese, a light white miso gets the right balance of flavour boost without overpowering.

... BUT NOT EVERY DISH BENEFITS

Much as I love to advocate for miso, I admit that some dishes are better off without it.

The first family of dishes are curries that contain aromatic spices such as cardamom, turmeric, cumin or coriander seeds; these can be dulled by the flavours of miso. Some tomato-based curries are made richer with a touch of miso, but my general rule is to not use it in curry dishes where you want the melody of spices to be the main feature. The umami effect distracts from the key role the spices are playing.

The second group of recipes in which miso doesn't work too well are those that are lacking in umami. For instance, fish and chips: the lack of umami in the dish means that miso would stand out too much and would no longer be a secret weapon.

THE SECRET WEAPON FOR TOMATO

It is hard to imagine the role that miso might play with tomato, until you break down tomato flavour to its constituent parts and consider how we cook with them generally.

The most optimum flavours come from the ripest tomatoes in season, but for all the other seasons of the year, we make do with concentrated versions, such as purée, passata or sun-dried tomatoes, where the purest elements of tomato are intensified by removing excess water. And even then, tomato flavours need seasoning; in Italian cooking, a pinch of bicarbonate of soda or sugar is added to reduce acidity and push the sweetness. In Spanish cuisine, red wine vinegar – another fermented ingredient with umami – is added to bring out the sweetness, as well as giving depth. Miso can do all three jobs and more. Adding miso to tomatoes brings out their sweetness, adds deeper notes and smooths over any acidity when a tomato sauce just does not taste tomatoey enough.

What's more, miso emulsifies sauces, so any watery elements in your tomato dish are rendered silky-smooth, adding a meaty depth that feels rich in the mouth, due to the kokumi effect (see page 189), plus the sauce will never split. The overall impact is truly sensational.

So many dishes start with a can of tomatoes; whether it is your favourite spaghetti sauce, a stew or a soup, adding a touch of miso to tomato-based dishes is magical. Miso makes the tomato flavour sing fuller and for longer, so when we can't harvest our tomatoes in San Marzano at the height of summer, miso is there to lift all your tomato dishes up on to their toes.

ULTIMATE PASTA ALLA NORMA

SERVES 2

1 medium aubergine (eggplant)
5 tbsp olive oil
1 small onion, finely chopped
3 fat garlic cloves, minced or finely grated
400 g/14 oz can of tomatoes
1 tbsp red wine vinegar
pinch of chilli (chile) flakes
200g dried spaghetti, or dried linguine
1 tbsp white miso
3 basil leaves, roughly torn, plus more to serve
sea salt and freshly ground black pepper

To serve
Parmesan cheese, or vegetarian Parmesan-style cheese
extra virgin olive oil

TIP: You can substitute tomato passata (strained tomatoes) for the can of tomatoes, if that's what you have in your kitchen cupboard. The resulting sauce will be a little smoother.

Once you realize that tomato sauces are enhanced with miso, you won't be able to grab a can of tomatoes from your cupboard without a jar of miso coming out too. This is the best veggie pasta ever; we know miso loves aubergines (see page 59), so the miso + aubergine + tomato triumvirate is a champion dish.

This is my favourite lazy-night pasta dish, when I am tired and just want something reliable and comforting. All you need is an aubergine and some store cupboard essentials.

And don't just stop at this pasta: add a spoon of miso to spaghetti bolognese, penne arrabbiata and all your tomatoey pasta bakes.

Chop the aubergine into bite-sized pieces. Heat 2–3 tbsp of the oil in a large frying pan (skillet) over a medium heat, then fry the aubergine until charred and succulently cooked through. Aubergines love oil, so don't be shy. This should take about 15 minutes and it is important not to rush it, to ensure you have juicy aubergine pieces. Take the aubergine out to rest and season with a pinch of salt and pepper.

In the same pan, warm up 2 tbsp more olive oil over a medium heat and add the onion and garlic, to cook down, soften and become slightly sticky. Then add the can of tomatoes and bring to a simmer, before stirring through the red wine vinegar and chilli flakes.

Meanwhile, in a large saucepan of boiling salted water, cook the spaghetti according to the packet instructions to al dente, reserving a small cup of the pasta-cooking liquid before draining.

Scoop out some of the tomato liquid into a small bowl and mix in the white miso with a small spoon until completely smooth and emulsified. Then add it all back into the pot of tomato sauce and stir through.

Add the aubergine and basil leaves to the sauce and warm through for 1 minute before adding the pasta, too. If the sauce is a little too thick, stir in some of the pasta-cooking water, to create a silkier sauce.

To finish, serve with the grated cheese, a drizzle of extra virgin olive oil and a basil leaf.

HARISSA SWEETCORN BAKED RICE

SERVES 8–10

2 tbsp olive oil
2 onions, finely chopped
2 garlic cloves, minced or finely grated
1 litre/1¾ pints tomato passata (strained tomatoes)
2 tbsp red wine vinegar
1 tbsp balsamic vinegar
3½ tbsp red miso
2½ tbsp rose harissa paste
1 tbsp maple syrup
finely grated zest of ½ lemon
400 g/14 oz frozen sweetcorn
400 g/14 oz arborio rice
600 ml/1 pint hot water

To serve
handful of finely chopped fresh parsley leaves
extra virgin olive oil

I credit this amazing dish to Henry Russell, a wonderful chef who I worked with to develop a miso harissa sauce. He probably won't even recall making it, as it was something he quickly created for our lunch, but I remember every mouthful. The rice is saturated with sweet tomato-pepper flavours, punctuated with refreshing pops of sweetcorn. It reminds me of a peppery jollof rice.

I went home that evening, re-made it immediately and have been perfecting the balance of flavours ever since. It's a crowd-pleasing dish that hits the spot when you have a group to feed and you need a solid, filling side dish that everyone, including vegetarians, can tuck into. It is great with roast fish, seafood or meats – especially fatty cuts such as lamb, pork chops or chicken thighs – or simply on its own with a fried egg on top and a drizzle of chilli (chile) oil for extra punch. Feel free to halve the recipe to serve four people, if you prefer.

The two vinegars do different jobs: the red wine vinegar adds depth to the sweet tomatoes, while the balsamic adds its sweetness.

You will need a heavy casserole (Dutch oven).

First, warm the olive oil in a frying pan (skillet) and soften the onions and garlic. When the onions are translucent, add the passata, both vinegars and miso, harissa paste, maple syrup and lemon zest.

Add the frozen corn and cook for 2 minutes until the corn is warmed through and coated in the peppery sauce.

Wash the rice, then add it to a heavy-based casserole and cover with the measured hot water. Next pour the tomato sauce into the rice and give it a good stir. Cover and bake in the oven for 20 minutes with the lid on until piping hot and the rice has absorbed the liquid. Continue cooking a further 20 minutes with the lid off: a charred crispy top will form on top of the rice. It should be sticky and sweet, with some extra sauce. As it cools, it will dry out and intensify in flavour. Finish with finely chopped parsley and a drizzle of extra virgin olive oil.

THE BEST BLOODY MARY

SERVES 2

600 ml/1 pint tomato juice
1½ tbsp white miso
4 dashes of Worcestershire sauce
4 dashes of Tabasco sauce
60 ml/2¼ fl oz vodka
ice cubes
2 celery sticks (optional)
2 lemon or lime wedges (optional)
freshly ground black pepper

Everyone who loves a Bloody Mary knows that there is a special knack to getting the best balance of rich tomato, sweetness, sharpness and spice. Get it right and it is juicy, satisfying and punchy, but get one ingredient off balance and you miss the spot!

My recipe is subtle; you cannot taste the miso in a big way. Instead, the tomato has more depth and roundness and the umami notes sing out for much longer. The miso smooths some of the spiky citrus and pepper notes, perfecting the balance in this drink impeccably.

Pour one-quarter of the tomato juice into a large jug, then mix in the miso paste until smooth. Top up with the remaining tomato juice. Add the Worcestershire sauce, Tabasco sauce, a pinch of black pepper and the vodka.

Stir or shake until fully combined, then add the ice cubes.

Carefully add a celery stick and squeeze in a lemon or lime wedge, if you like, then serve.

THE SECRET WEAPON FOR CHEESE

If you love cheesy dishes, then adding miso to them gives you cheese-on-steroids every time. Since cheese, like miso, is also a deeply flavoured aged ingredient, they have lived parallel lives in the east and west, both powerful products of fermentation and great sources of umami. Pair them together and – wow – the combination is outstanding.

THE ULTIMATE MAC AND CHEESE

SERVES 6–8 GENEROUSLY

---

60 g/2¼ oz unsalted butter
60 g/2¼ oz plain (all-purpose) flour
600 ml/1 pint full-fat milk
100 g/3½ oz Gruyère cheese, grated
100 g/3½ oz Cheddar cheese, grated
100 g/3½ oz Cheshire cheese, grated
1 tsp smoked paprika
2 tsp English mustard powder
1 tbsp white miso
200 g/7 oz white crabmeat, canned or fresh (optional)
50 g/1¾ oz finely chopped fresh chives (optional)
120 g/4¼ oz dried macaroni pasta
sea salt and freshly ground black pepper

For the topping (optional)
½ tsp fresh thyme leaves, finely chopped
½ tsp finely chopped fresh parsley leaves
50 g/1¾ oz panko crumbs

TIP: You can also add other seafoods, such as prawns (shrimp) or crayfish (crawfish).

This cheese sauce is on another level. Not only has it got three different cheeses, each bringing its own qualities – creamy sweetness from Cheddar, acidity from Cheshire and nuttiness from Gruyère – but miso's role here provides one of the most impressive makeovers I have tasted in a home-cooked dish. Adding miso to cheese makes it taste as though you added a lot more cheese than you did, miraculously giving more flavour without more fat. I also tend to add crab and chive for extra flavour and freshness.

First make a roux. Melt the butter in a heavy-based saucepan over a medium heat, then add the flour slowly until a paste forms. Keep moving it around in the pan to allow for the flour rawness to be cooked out and the flour to reach a golden colour.

Now begin to add the milk slowly, carefully mixing the roux into the milk to create a creamy sauce. If you add the milk too fast, the flour will form lumps, so be patient!

Once all the milk is added and is warmed through, add all three cheeses, which will melt in to create a thick sauce. Season with a couple of grinds of salt and pepper.

Take a cup of sauce out of the pot and in a small bowl, whisk in the paprika, mustard powder and miso to create a thick but smooth paste. Now pour it back into the pan to mix in fully with the body of the sauce. Switch the heat off: you now have your cheese sauce. It will have a slight pink hue which will turn golden on cooking.

Now add the crab and chopped chives (if using).

Preheat the oven to 180°C fan/200°C/400°F/gas mark 6.

Boil the macaroni in salted boiling water according to the packet instructions, then drain and rinse. Combine with the cheese sauce and spoon into an ovenproof dish, then bake for 20 minutes.

If you are adding the topping, mix the herbs and panko in a bowl, then sprinkle evenly over the macaroni. Bake for a further 15–20 minutes until the topping is golden brown.

BEST EVER TRIPLE UMAMI LASAGNE

SERVES 6

12 dried lasagne sheets

For the ragu
2 tbsp olive oil
2 onions, peeled and finely chopped
6 garlic cloves, minced or finely grated
400 g/14 oz minced (ground) pork with at least 5 percent fat
400 g/14 oz minced (ground) beef with at least 5 percent fat
1.35 litres/2¼ pints (2 regular bottles) tomato passata (strained tomatoes)
70 g/2½ oz rose harissa paste
1 tbsp red wine vinegar, ideally Merlot
60 g/2¼ oz white miso
handful of basil leaves, plus more for the top
salt and freshly ground black pepper

For the white sauce
30 g/1 oz unsalted butter
2 tbsp plain (all-purpose) flour
500 ml/18 fl oz full-fat milk
100 g/3½ oz mature Cheddar cheese, or Gruyère cheese, grated
freshly grated nutmeg
2 tbsp white miso

If you know that miso boosts tomato, and you know that miso boosts cheese, imagine the combo in a lasagne, with a double helping of our favourite umami flavour booster.

This recipe has been honed for years in my home and, whenever I make it, my partner cannot leave it alone! Expect an empty dish and requests for seconds, and make sure you make more than you think you need!

If you already have a much-loved lasagne recipe, then you can simply upgrade it by adding the miso to the tomato base as well as to the cheese sauce. And don't just stop at lasagne, think of all the dishes you make that contain both tomato and cheese: pizza sauce, spaghetti bolognese and moussaka.

My lasagne recipe is made with minced (ground) beef and pork, but I have included a version with tuna, anchovy and lentils for pescatarians, or with mushrooms and lentils for vegetarians (see Tip, overleaf). If you are making it with minced meat, go for 5 percent fat for extra richness. The rose harissa in my recipe brings warmth to the dish without the distraction that spiky fresh chilli (chile) would provide.

Delicious served with a green salad with tomatoes and some olive oil and vinegar and a chunk of crusty garlic bread.

In a large frying pan (skillet) over a medium heat, warm up the olive oil and cook the onions for 5 minutes. Add the garlic, reduce the heat and cook until the onions are softened. Add the meat and cook for 10 minutes, then add the passata and simmer for 5 minutes.

In a small bowl, mix together the harissa, red wine vinegar and miso paste, then pour this into the sauce. Add a small grind of salt and pepper, tear the basil into the sauce and turn off the heat.

Continues overleaf

TIP: This is a very versatile recipe and can suit many different dietary requirements. Simply replace the minced meat in the recipe above with:

- For a fish lasagne, use 400 g/14 oz jarred or canned tuna, 200 g/7 oz cooked Puy (French) lentils and 2 chopped anchovies. Cook in the pan with the onions for just 3 minutes, then continue as for the main recipe.
- For a veggie lasagne, use 700 g/1 lb 9 oz chopped chestnut (cremini) mushrooms, 200 g/7 oz cooked Puy (French) lentils and 2 tsp roughly chopped capers. Cook in the pan with the onions for 10 minutes, as for the main recipe, then continue.

To make the white sauce, in a separate heavy-based saucepan over a low heat, melt the butter before adding the flour and stirring until it forms a soft smooth paste. Keep moving it in the pan to prevent it from burning. Now gradually add the milk, slowly at first, to create a sauce. Melt the cheese into the hot sauce and stir through, then add a pinch of nutmeg, salt and pepper to season and switch off the heat.

Scoop a few tablespoons of the white sauce into a small bowl, then mix in the miso paste. Once it is smooth, pour it back into the remaining white sauce. It will give it a light caramel colour.

Prepare the pasta sheets according to the packet instructions.

Preheat the oven to 190°C fan/210°C/410°F/gas mark 6½.

To build the lasagne, spoon one-third of the ragu into a large deep ovenproof dish (roughly 35 x 25 cm/14 x 10 in) and spread it out evenly. Spoon over one-third of the white sauce, then layer on the first layer of lasagne sheets, making sure they fully cover the sauce in a single layer. Repeat this for a second layer of sauces and pasta, then finish with a final layer of ragu and white sauce and a few basil leaves.

Bake in the oven for 35–45 minutes until golden and bubbling. Remove the lasagne from the oven and leave to sit for 5–10 minutes before serving.

THE GREATEST TUNA CHEESE TOASTIE

SERVES 4

250 g/9 oz jarred or canned tuna in oil
1 small garlic clove, finely minced or grated
1 tsp peeled and finely grated root ginger
2 spring onions (scallions), finely chopped
4 tbsp white miso
unsalted butter, for the bread
8 slices of sourdough, or your favourite type of bread
200 g/7 oz Cheddar cheese, grated
a little oil, for the griddle (grill) pan (optional)

TIP: If you have some of the tuna mix left over, whizz it up into a smooth pâté in a food processor and serve in ramekins with toasted bread, pickles and raw vegetables for a light snack or starter (appetizer).

If you love a good tuna melt, as I do, the umami scores here are off the charts. Use good-quality jarred tuna for the best results. This is a quick and easy store cupboard snack that still feels special.

Simply put the tuna, garlic, ginger, spring onions and miso into a small bowl and mix thoroughly. Butter the bread on both sides and then spread the tuna mixture on one side of half the bread slices. Now layer the cheese generously over the tuna. Top with the pieces of plain buttered bread.

Place each sandwich on a lightly oiled, preheated hot griddle (grill) pan over a medium-high heat, pressing down and cooking for 2 minutes on each side before serving, or simply use a toasted sandwich maker. The cheese should be melted and dripping before serving.

THE SECRET WEAPON FOR ONIONS

Boosting the humble onion is a great way to showcase the magic of miso. This is not a new idea, in fact Yotam Ottolenghi created a wonderful dish called miso butter onions: he roasts a tray of onions in a miso emulsion, wrapped in foil parcels, at a high heat. The result is an impressive low-effort but high-impact dish: the onions become a caramel colour with translucent silky petals dripping in moreish miso butter.

Whether onions are cooked slowly, or at a high heat, the Maillard reaction occurs between the sugar and amino acids, which yields a lot of flavour and gives that characteristic caramelized colour and taste. The sweet flavours of the onions are then made more complex when contrasted against miso's umami savoury notes. You will experience that sweet-savoury flavour combination that our palates love.

ULTIMATE FRENCH ONION SOUP

SERVES 4–6

---

30 g/1 oz plain (all-purpose) flour
60 g/2¼ oz unsalted butter
1 kg/2 lb 4 oz onions, very finely sliced on a mandoline or by hand
10 g/¼ oz sea salt
2 pinches of freshly ground black pepper
200 ml/7 fl oz dry white wine
1 tbsp red miso, plus more if needed
1 tbsp white miso, plus more if needed
1–1.5 litres/1¾–2¾ pints hot water

The best French onion soups are deep in flavour, the onions are translucent and sweet and a touch boozy. The most important ingredients, though, are time and some good stock. Onions need to be slow cooked for an almost painful amount of time in order to caramelize. Beef stock is typically needed to add the depth we crave.

But what if you don't eat beef? You guessed it: miso to the rescue. Adding red miso to onion-based dishes brings a meaty depth which is otherwise impossible to replicate with vegetarian ingredients, or achieve in this short cooking time. This is something I love to make on special occasions.

First toast the flour in a small dry saucepan over a low heat for 10 minutes, keeping the flour moving in the pan. It should turn from white to a creamy colour. Set aside.

Next, in a large saucepan or casserole (Dutch oven), melt the butter over a medium heat, then add one-quarter of the onions and cook until softened, before adding another one-quarter. Continue in this fashion to cook all the onions, keeping them moving. It will take about 1 hour until the onions are brown, caramelized, very soft and considerably reduced in volume. This is the step that will make your onion soup really silky.

When you are ready to finish the soup, season with the salt and pepper, then add the toasted flour, stirring to coat the onions. Pour in the white wine, bring to a simmer and cook for 5 minutes.

Scoop 2 tbsp of the liquid from the pan and mix it in a small bowl with the red and white miso pastes, before pouring it back into the pan. This prevents lumps in the soup.

Finally, add 500 ml/18 fl oz of the measured hot water to the onion base, then up to a further 500 ml/18 fl oz. If you like an even thinner broth, add a final 500 ml/18 fl oz water, a little at a time, until you get the consistency you are looking for.

Check the seasoning. Add more red miso if you want more depth, or more white miso for more sweetness, but take care not to add too much: the miso flavour should not dominate.

BEST EVER GRAVY

Some meals are not worth even thinking about if you can't nail a great gravy. Think of sausages and mash, the Sunday roast, or pie and chips (fries). But gravy can be just a little too thin, or too light in flavour, when what you want is a deep liquor that brings a dish together.

These two variations are foolproof, whether you want a meaty or a veggie gravy; both have the rich and silky texture you desire. The miso brings a depth of flavour, supercharging those sweet caramelized notes in the onions. It also helps to thicken the gravy too, as the lecithin in the soya beans naturally emulsifies the sauces without recourse to cornflour (cornstarch). Once you have made gravy with miso, you won't go back!

VEGETARIAN OR VEGAN CARAMELIZED ONION GRAVY

SERVES 6

50 g/1¾ oz unsalted butter, or vegan alternative
2 onions, thinly sliced
2 tbsp plain (all-purpose) flour
120 ml/4 fl oz red wine (vegetarian or vegan, if needed)
leaves from 2 fresh thyme sprigs
4 tbsp red miso
750 ml/1¼ pints hot water
½ tsp English mustard powder
1 tbsp balsamic vinegar
sea salt and freshly ground black pepper

Melt the butter in a saucepan over a medium-high heat, then reduce the heat to low, add the onions and cook for about 30 minutes until they are caramelized. Add the flour and mix it into the onions.

Next add the red wine and thyme: the onions will take on the red colour of the wine.

Put the miso in a small bowl and gradually whisk in the measured hot water until it has dissolved.

Add the miso broth slowly, whisking to prevent lumps from forming, then add the mustard and some salt and pepper and bring to the boil. Cover and simmer for 20 minutes. Add the vinegar to finish.

BEEF AND ONION GRAVY

SERVES 6

beef juices, from the roast beef roasting tin
2 onions, thinly sliced
50 g/1¾ oz plain (all-purpose) flour
200 ml/7 fl oz red wine
leaves from 2 fresh thyme sprigs
4 tbsp red miso
750 ml/1¼ pints hot water
sea salt and freshly ground black pepper

Decant the beef juices from the roasting tin into a wide pan, set over a low heat and simmer for 5 minutes, before adding the onions. Cook for 20–25 minutes until the onions are super-soft and the liquor has darkened.

Stir in the flour until combined and then whisk in the red wine, making sure there are no lumps. Add the thyme. Bring to the boil, whisking, then increase the heat so that the wine is reduced by about half.

Put the miso in a small bowl and gradually whisk in the measured hot water until it has dissolved.

Whisk the red miso broth into the gravy, then cook over a medium heat for about 8 minutes, stirring occasionally, until you have a thickened sauce. Taste and adjust the seasoning, then serve.

UMAMIFIED SUNDAY ROAST

While I don't recommend putting miso in every dish (see 'Toomami', page 33), having one or two elements of a roast containing a miso booster is plenty for upgrading your feast. When I make a roast at home, you can bet I have my secret ingredient on standby. So here are my tips for umamifying your Sunday roast, but of course each element can be enjoyed as dishes in their own right throughout the week too.

MISO GLAZE FOR ROAST CHICKEN, OR PORK LOIN

110 g/4 oz white miso
1 tbsp toasted sesame oil
1 tbsp soy sauce
1 tbsp runny honey
finely grated zest of ½ lemon

Simply mix all the ingredients together and brush on to meat before cooking it in the usual way.

MISO RUB FOR BEEF, LAMB, DUCK OR GAMEY MEATS

150 g/5½ oz red miso
1 tbsp toasted sesame oil
½ tsp 5-spice
1½ tbsp runny honey
1 tbsp olive oil

Simply mix all the ingredients together and rub on to meat before cooking it in the usual way.

Pictured overleaf

MISO GLAZED CARROTS OR SQUASH

ENOUGH FOR 450 G/1 LB CARROTS OR 400 G/14 OZ SQUASH

2 tbsp white miso
2 tbsp runny honey
1 tbsp olive oil
a little vegetable oil

Simply mix together the miso, honey and olive oil in a small bowl to create a sticky miso glaze. Peel and chop your vegetables, then roast for half their total cooking time with just a little vegetable oil. Brush on the glaze at this halfway point, to ensure that it stays on the vegetables and that the sweet glaze does not burn. Finish in the oven for the remainder of the cooking time until golden and caramelized.

MISO BUTTER PEAS OR SPINACH

Simply steam or boil your peas according to the packet instructions, or wilt your spinach in a warm pan, then place a knob of my Basic Miso Butter (see page 126) on top to melt.

MISO BUTTER ROAST POTATOES

SERVES 4

1 kg/2 lb 4 oz potatoes
3 tbsp white miso
4 tbsp unsalted butter, softened to room temperature
2 tbsp vegetable oil
handful of chopped fresh tarragon leaves, or chopped fresh chives (optional)
sea salt and freshly ground black pepper

These carry such a deep, rich flavour that you would be forgiven for thinking they have been laced with duck fat or beef dripping. Vegetarian-friendly and astonishingly good, they reheat well too, in the unlikely event of any going spare.

Peel the potatoes and cut into roastie-sized pieces. Boil in a saucepan of salted water until fully cooked through, but not yet breaking apart. Drain into a large colander and, with a plate on top, give the potatoes a good shake to rough up the edges. Remove the plate and let the potatoes cool for a few minutes.

Meanwhile, in a small bowl, whisk up the miso, butter and oil into an emulsion with a few grinds of black pepper, adding the herbs for another layer of flavour, if you like.

Preheat the oven to 200°C fan/220°C/425°F/gas mark 7.

Lay your cooked potatoes on 2 baking trays, leaving as much space as you can between them. With a pastry brush, paint the potatoes with all the miso butter, or spoon it carefully over each potato. Season with more pepper.

Roast for 30–35 minutes until golden and crispy, watching carefully so the miso does not burn, though some bits will char.

MISO SESAME YORKSHIRE PUDDINGS

MAKES 12

100 g/3½ oz plain (all-purpose) flour
½ tsp English mustard powder
3 large eggs
220 ml/8 fl oz full-fat milk
1 tsp white miso
2 tsp toasted sesame seeds
1 tbsp toasted sesame oil
3 tbsp vegetable oil

As I spent my junior years in Yorkshire, these hunky gems have a special place in my heart. The miso sesame flavour twist is inspired by a business in London called Ling Lings, which serves incredible Asian-inspired Sunday roasts; I am a massive fan.

Preheat the oven to 200°C fan/220°C/425°F/gas mark 7.

In a large bowl, mix the flour and mustard powder, then make a well in the centre. Beat in the eggs and a little of the milk. Whisk until smooth, add the miso paste and sesame seeds and whisk again until smooth. Slowly whisk in the rest of the milk.

Mix the oils together and then measure 1 tsp into each hole of a 12-hole bun tin. Place in the oven for 5 minutes to get the oil super-hot.

Carefully remove the tin from the oven and pour the batter equally into each of the holes. Return to the oven and cook for 20–25 minutes or until golden brown and risen.

ADD A SPOON AND SEE!

So many of our favourite comfort dishes start with the softening of an onion. Think cottage pie, beef bourguignon, any kind of savoury pies, or lentil- and bean-based bakes. As the weather cools, we think of stews, chillis and slow-cooked hot pots, all of which start with an onion. Miso is a game-changer for all these dishes, adding richness as well as thickening and rounding-off flavours.

Instead of giving you recipes for all these home-cooked classics, I encourage you to 'add a spoon and see'.

If you are cooking for two people, start by adding 1 tsp of miso at a time at the end of your seasoning, before a dish goes in the oven, or before serving. If you are cooking for three or more, add 1 tbsp of miso at a time until you get the desired effect. In all cases, take care not to add too much miso: you shouldn't be able to taste it at all. Instead, you will notice how all the flavours gather, as if they are more closely related to one another.

As a general rule, white miso is better suited for dishes with a tomato element, and red miso when there is an onion base but no tomato. However, feel free to experiment as well, to suit your taste.

So that is your mission: add a spoon and see. You will discover what a magic wand miso can be in your kitchen, creating a special halo around all your favourite dishes. I promise you won't go back.

THE ULTIMATE KITCHEN HERO

Once you discover that your most-loved dishes are better with miso, it will become essential in your life, as it has become for me. May it sit at the front of your cupboard or refrigerator, or next to your oven alongside the salt and pepper, always ready for action. I hope it will gain a regular well-earned spot on your shopping list.

But I should give you a warning: your new-found knowledge can sadly ruin your experience of eating other people's cooking! Your tastebuds are clever: once they learn how good a dish can taste, it is hard to go back. Any dishes I order in a restaurant with a tomato or cheese base often lack the level of oomph that miso brings when I cook them at home, and no amount of salt and pepper I add at the table will correct this. I have been known to bring my own miso to restaurants and subtly stir it in, but I have yet to go so far as to do the same at a dinner party.

SO... HOW DOES IT WORK?

1. MULTIPLYING UMAMI LEVELS

To understand what is truly happening here, we have to go back to what we have already learned about umami. Umami is the fifth taste together with sweet, salt, sour and bitter, a flavour that is deeply savoury with its own receptor system on your tongue. It can also influence the other taste receptors, such is its power.

Miso, as a fermented material, encourages the enzymic breakdown of soya, which yields amino acids (glutamic acid and aspartic acid) known to stimulate the umami effect on our taste receptors. In turn, we perceive their level of stimulation as exciting and simply cannot get enough of it. It's an almost addictive sensation on the tongue, which the brain detects as pleasurable. (This effect is also the basic principle behind the original design of MSG.)

But miso does more than enhance savoury flavours, it also alters flavour perception, which is part of its umami-multiplying power. Often, when we are providing the finishing touches to a dish, we taste it and notice something missing: it needs more 'oomph'. We may once have reached for more salt, more butter, more cheese or more stock. But adding miso is a far better move, as you are not just layering on more flavour, but you are adding umami. This takes the elements of the dish at a chemical level and supercharges their flavours by multiplying their detectable glutamates and thereby delivering more flavour from the *existing* ingredients. *You are making the existing ingredients work harder.*

2. THE KOKUMI EFFECT

Something else is happening when we experience this miso-boosting trick. In fact, this is perhaps the most exciting part of miso acting as a secret weapon. Adding miso delivers a specific mouthfeel: the whole mouth fills with a richness and body that is quite extraordinary. In all the dishes in this chapter, flavours will not only be deeper, but taste sensations will be transformative: your tongue will feel softly coated in flavour that lingers and echoes in your mouth like a chamber filled with music. It sounds dramatic, because it really is sensational. Often what we are seeking, when we are tasting and seasoning our meals, is not just more depth of flavour but also texture; we want more layers and tones. Solo artists are wonderful with their stripped-back charms, but when it comes to cooking, an orchestra of flavour is what really hits the spot.

The kokumi effect (see page 19) has been novel and magical for me. Adding miso not only affects our perception of flavour, but also – remarkably – our perception of *texture*. Remember, the Japanese concept of kokumi comes from the words *koko* meaning 'body' and *mi* meaning 'flavour'.

The effect is helpful in understanding the difference between saltiness and umami, which are often confused because we do not have the language to describe the difference. When you taste salt, the zingy flavour hits your mouth in a sharp spike and then disappears, often leaving you with a dry mouth. With umami, the flavour lingers and holds on: the kokumi effect stretches out gently like a song you don't want to end. If you want to try it for yourself, put salt on your tongue: the flavour hit lasts up to five seconds, then you are left with a dry mouth, while miso lasts 15–20 seconds in your mouth and lingers softly.

This is at the heart of why miso is the ultimate ingredient: there is no other that can deliver such a multitude of flavour and texture sensations.

THE SECRET WEAPON FOR COCOA

Miso and cocoa might strike you as an unexpected pairing for flavour boosting, but if you have ever added salt to a chocolate dessert, or dropped a square of chocolate into a Tex-Mex chilli, you will know that chocolate can behave in unexpected ways in sweet and savoury dishes.

Adding miso to a cocoa dish brings balance to any outstanding sweetness, yes, but it's about more than that. Just as cheese, tomato and onions have a level of umami that can be boosted by miso, so does cocoa. Remember: cocoa is itself a fermented bean; it contains its own naturally occurring glutamates which can be enhanced by miso in an extraordinary way.

I often hold blind tastings of hot chocolate with and without miso. When you taste hot chocolate with miso (see page 195), you will enjoy the familiar indulgent sweetness, but suddenly it tastes more luxurious, thicker, richer and the flavour sings for much longer. If you then go back to hot chocolate without miso, it will taste overly sweet and thinner on the palate, because of the kokumi effect (see page 189). I really hope you give this simple application a go: miso and cocoa are a match made in dessert heaven.

ULTIMATE CHOCOLATE BROWNIES

SERVES 6–8

- 170 g/6 oz good-quality 70 percent cocoa solids chocolate
- 170 g/6 oz unsalted butter, chopped
- 250 g/9 oz caster (superfine) sugar
- 3 eggs
- 1 large tbsp white miso
- 115 g/4 oz plain (all-purpose) flour
- 50 g/1¾ oz walnuts, roughly chopped (optional)

These are so much a part of me that I even baked them for my wedding day. As soon as you bite into their rich density, you will be hit with a deep, buttery, powerful chocolate punch: all the hallmarks of a brownie, but taken to new heights. The miso adds subtle caramel notes and the cocoa flavours linger so much that you cannot resist going immediately for a second bite.

You cannot detect a strong miso flavour, instead the taste of the chocolate is intensified. These are very rich, so are best cut into small bite-sized chunks, or eaten together with crème fraîche, whipped cream or good-quality vanilla ice cream.

You will need a 20 cm/8 in square baking tin (pan).

Preheat the oven to 160°C fan/180°C/350°F/gas mark 4. Line a 20 cm/8 in square brownie tin with baking paper (parchment paper).

Set a heatproof bowl over a saucepan of simmering water set over a medium heat. Break the chocolate into the bowl and melt it with the butter into a thick sauce. Remove from the pan to cool.

In a medium bowl, whisk together the sugar and eggs with electric beaters until it foams. Now mix in the chocolatey butter to combine.

To add the miso, scoop 2 tablespoons of the batter into a small bowl and blend in the miso paste until completely smooth. Pour it all back into the main bowl of brownie batter and stir together well. Stir in the flour and the walnuts, if using.

Pour the batter into the prepared tin. Bake for 18–21 minutes, then remove from the oven. Leave to cool for 5 minutes before transferring to a cooling rack, still in a single piece and inside the baking paper that lined the tin. It will stay a little fragile until completely cooled and will have a soft fudgy consistency inside.

Serve with crème fraîche, whipped cream or ice cream, or with a hot cup of coffee.

THE GREATEST CHOCOLATE MOUSSE

SERVES 6

100 g/3½ oz good-quality 70 percent cocoa solids chocolate, chopped
100 g/3½ oz milk chocolate, chopped
2 tsp white miso
150 ml/5 fl oz double (heavy) cream
4 large egg whites
80 g/3 oz caster (superfine) sugar
40 g/1½ oz pistachios or walnuts, chopped (optional)
sour cherry molasses, to serve (optional)

A quick and easy dessert that can be made a day in advance. Smooth and silky, it tastes decadent and the cocoa flavours are supercharged with white miso.

Set a heatproof bowl over a saucepan of simmering water set over a medium heat. Break the 2 chocolates into the bowl and melt them. Remove from the pan to cool. You can also melt the chocolate in a microwave in 25-second bursts, giving it a quick stir between each.

In a large separate bowl, combine the miso and cream and beat them together using electric beaters until soft peaks have formed. This will take about 5 minutes.

In a clean bowl, mix together the egg whites and sugar with the electric beaters (make sure you clean your beaters in between), until thick and holding its shape.

Gently fold the chocolate into the miso cream. Then, a large spoon at a time, fold the egg whites into the chocolate cream. Take care not to knock the air out of the mix.

Divide the mixture between 6 glasses or ramekins and chill for at least 4 hours or overnight. Take the mousse out of the refrigerator 20 minutes before serving, sprinkled with chopped nuts and sour cherry molasses, if you like.

THE BEST HOT CHOCOLATE

SERVES 2

2 tsp white miso
2 tbsp maple syrup
2 tbsp cocoa powder
2 tbsp dark (bittersweet) chocolate, grated
500 ml/18 fl oz oat milk, or dairy milk, if you prefer

TIP: To give your hot chocolate some extra zing, consider adding a grating of peeled root ginger or pinch of ground cinnamon. Of course, marshmallows are always welcome too.

I love a hot chocolate but would not usually order it when I'm out, because hot chocolate without a touch of miso is seriously missing a trick. Once you have tried this recipe, all others will feel lacking in depth of flavour. The miso brings a salted caramel flavour which lingers and stops the drink from tasting too sweet, elevating a basic hot chocolate into an indulgence.

You can of course simply add 1 tsp white miso to regular instant hot chocolate at home, but if you want to go to a little more effort and make a drink without refined sugars, here is your recipe! This is a decadent treat that is both pure and naturally vegan.

Put the miso paste in a small bowl and stir in the maple syrup, cocoa powder, grated chocolate and a splash of the oat milk to create a paste.

Next, warm up the remaining milk in a saucepan, then slowly pour in the miso chocolate paste, whisking all the time, to dissolve into the milk. This stops any lumps from forming.

Once it starts to bubble, reduce the heat and serve.

For most of its history, miso has been a key player in delivering savoury, umami-rich flavours to Japanese cuisine, alongside its flavour-boosting sibling shoyu (Japanese soy sauce).

Today, miso's growing prevalence in desserts – both in Japan and around the world – has marked a shift in perception by chefs who see its potential in sweet food. Miso adds complexity and a Japanese accent to desserts. This is fusion cooking at its finest, mixing ingredients from different cultures in inventive ways that our tastebuds love.

The power of miso to balance sweetness and add depth has inspired many pastry chefs and home bakers to use it as a twist in their creations, which dance between sweet and savoury notes, an utterly stimulating package for the senses.

The key to using miso in sweet dishes is to do so sparingly. It should not be the main flavour you can taste, more a supporting act than the leading role.

As miso does not melt with heat, it can contribute to a more fudgy texture too, which is a lovely surprise in cakes, traybakes and chewy American-style cookies, but tends to work less well in biscuits (cracker-style cookies), when you want a clean snappy bite.

If you are new to making desserts with miso, I recommend you start with lighter versions, such as white miso or a young barley miso, which both work their magic brilliantly on creamy desserts. Darker misos have a funkiness to them that takes some getting used to, but work well alongside citrus or spice notes.

THE DESSERT TWIST

WHITE MISO ICE CREAM WITH HAZELNUT PRALINE

SERVES 6

For the ice cream
250 ml/9 fl oz full-fat milk
100 g/3½ oz caster (superfine) sugar
400 ml/14 fl oz double (heavy) cream
5 egg yolks
75 g/2¾ oz white miso

For the praline
a little flavourless oil
125 g/4½ oz golden caster (unrefined superfine) sugar
125 g/4½ oz hazelnuts

A classic ice cream recipe made more elegant with a miso twist and a hazelnut crunch. If you love salted-caramel anything, then this is a game-changer. Sweet and savoury in equal measure, I can get through an impressive amount of it in one sitting. The praline is a bit more extra work, but it is a winning touch.

Heat the milk and sugar in a heavy-based saucepan, stirring to help the sugar dissolve.

Make an ice bath by putting a 2-litre (3½-pint) metal or plastic bowl in a larger bowl partially filled with iced water. Place a sieve (strainer) above the bowl and pour in the cream.

In a different bowl, whisk the egg yolks and miso together until smooth.

Now slowly pour the warm milk mixture on to the yolks, whisking all the time. Scrape the mixture back into the saucepan and cook over a very low heat, stirring constantly with a spatula until the custard is thick enough to coat it.

Strain the custard through the sieve and into the double cream. Slowly stir over the ice until the custard is cooled, before refrigerating to completely chill it for a minimum of 3 hours.

Meanwhile, make the praline: lightly oil a baking sheet. In a dry, heavy-based saucepan, cook the sugar over a medium heat, stirring with a fork until it is all melted, then slowly cook without stirring until it is a golden caramel colour. Swirl the pan to keep it moving, then add the hazelnuts.

Immediately pour the mixture on to the prepared baking sheet and let it cool completely; this should take about 30 minutes. Break it into small pieces.

Once the ice cream and praline are thoroughly cooled, put the ice cream in an ice cream machine and churn according to the manufacturer's instructions, adding the praline right at the end of churning, so it stays in lovely chunks.

MISO BROWN BUTTER BANANA BREAD WITH MISO CUSTARD

SERVES 8–10

3 very ripe bananas
1½ tbsp white miso
180 g/6 oz unsalted butter
2 large eggs
100 g/3½ oz caster (superfine) sugar
handful of soft dried apricots, finely chopped
150 g/5½ oz self-raising (self-rising) flour
2½ tsp baking powder
handful of walnuts, roughly chopped

For the custard (optional)
Makes 1 litre/1¾ pints
200 ml/7 fl oz double (heavy) cream
700 ml/1¼ pints full-fat milk
4 large egg yolks
3 tbsp cornflour (cornstarch)
100 g/3½ oz caster (superfine) sugar
1 tbsp white miso

I have made this more than a hundred times and I will never stop. Chef Simon Rimmer said it was 'possibly the best pudding I have ever eaten', and the recipe has – somewhat accidentally – become my signature bake!

I love doing blind taste tests with this: I bake two banana breads, one with miso and one without. Consistently, the feedback has been that the loaf containing miso surely has more bananas, or that I have added caramel.

The beauty of miso here is that it draws out the ripe, almost fudgy, banana flavours and deepens them with butterscotch notes. By browning the butter first, it adds a deep nuttiness that complements the caramel flavours from the miso. This is a must-try: you will never make banana bread without miso again. If you don't like cakes too sweet, this one is for you.

Use the ripest bananas you can find. To elevate this loaf bake into a proper dessert for dinner, serve it with this miso custard. It's not only great with banana bread but also with all sponge cakes and even simply on its own, as it has a salted caramel flavour.

Preheat the oven to 160°C fan/180°C/350°F/gas mark 4. Line a 22 x 11 x 7 cm/9 x 4½ x 2½ in or 900 g/2 lb loaf tin (pan) with baking paper (parchment paper).

Break down 2 of the bananas with a potato masher or fork. Stir in the miso paste until well combined and smooth.

In a heavy-based saucepan, brown the butter over a medium heat for 4–5 minutes until it darkens to a caramel colour and you can smell a nutty aroma. It will bubble a bit and this is normal. Transfer the butter to a bowl to cool down.

In a large bowl, beat the eggs and sugar together with electric beaters until creamy and thick. Add the miso banana mix, apricots and cooled brown butter and stir until combined. Don't worry if there are small specks of brown in the butter, this will give you those caramel notes.

Sift the flour and baking powder into another bowl and make a small well in the middle. Slowly pour the wet mixture into the flour, beating gently to combine.

Pour the batter into the prepared tin and scatter the walnuts on top.

Finally, slice the final banana lengthways and lay both halves on top of the loaf tin, cut sides up.

Bake for 45–55 minutes until golden on top and a skewer comes out clean. Cool in the tin for 10 minutes before turning out on to a wire rack to cool completely.

If making the custard, put the cream and milk into a large saucepan and bring to the boil, before taking off the heat.

In a large bowl, whisk the egg yolks, cornflour and sugar into a smooth paste, then slowly add the miso and blend it in carefully. Take the hot milk mixture and pour it slowly into the sugar mixture, whisking constantly to ensure there are no lumps.

Pour all the mixture back into the saucepan and warm it up again over a low heat, where it will thicken from the cornflour. Take care not to overcook it at this stage, and warm it back up just before serving.

STEM GINGER AND BARLEY MISO CHEESECAKE

SERVES 8

200 g/7 oz digestive biscuits (graham crackers)
150 g/5½ oz unsalted butter, melted and cooled slightly
115 g/4 oz caster (superfine) sugar
500 g/1 lb 2 oz full-fat cream cheese
45 g/1½ oz barley miso
3 large eggs
50 g/1¾ oz stem (candied) ginger, sliced finely into small matchsticks
a little of the stem (candied) ginger syrup, to serve

I am not usually a fan of cheesecakes: I find them a little one-dimensional and usually too sweet. In this recipe, the twist is in the miso, to add depth and savouriness, while the sweet ginger also helps to cut through the richness. Barley miso brings a malty taste which makes it extra moreish.

You will need a 24 cm/9½ in springform tin (pan).

Preheat the oven to 160°C fan/180°C/350°F/gas mark 4.

To make the base, pulse the biscuits in a food processor into fine crumbs, then transfer to a medium bowl. Stir in the melted butter and mix until evenly distributed. Press the mixture into a 24 cm/9½ in springform tin (pan). Bake for 10 minutes, then remove from the oven and allow to cool.

Reduce the oven temperature to 140°C fan/160°C/325°F/gas mark 3.

Next, make the filling. In a large mixing bowl, beat the sugar and cream cheese using a wooden spoon or spatula, scraping down the sides of the bowl frequently, for 3–5 minutes until light and fluffy.

Add the miso slowly, 1 tbsp at a time, until evenly distributed, then beat in each egg separately, then, finally, the stem ginger pieces. Pour on to the base and bake for 1 hour.

Turn off the oven, open the door slightly and allow the cheesecake to cool slowly inside, to prevent cracking, for a further hour.

Chill in the refrigerator for at least 4 hours, before serving drizzled with ginger syrup.

POACHED PEARS WITH LEMON MISO SYRUP

SERVES 4

4 ripe pears
1 tbsp white miso
1 tbsp red miso
finely grated zest and juice of 1 lemon
500 ml/18 fl oz boiling water
2.5 cm/1 in root ginger, peeled and julienned
2 tbsp caster (superfine) sugar
4 tbsp light brown sugar
4 tbsp mascarpone (optional)

TIP: A little yogurt and a grating of lemon zest on the side would add even more freshness to this little number.

I love the elegance of poached pears, with their long necks and shiny bodies. The addition of the miso lemon syrup here brings a refreshing end to a heavy meal. A lovely dessert to make in advance, before heating up when you're ready to serve.

First, peel the pears carefully and slice off the bottoms so they have flat bases.

In a mixing bowl, combine both types of miso and the lemon zest and juice, then gradually pour in the measured boiling water, mixing until combined. Stir in the ginger.

Lay the pears in a heavy-based wide pan and pour the miso mixture on top. Place over a medium heat for 5 minutes, then add the caster sugar. Reduce the heat and poach for 45–60 minutes, until the pears are tender.

In a small separate saucepan, take 200 ml/7 fl oz of the pear-poaching liquid, add the brown sugar and heat for 10–15 minutes until a sticky thick syrup forms.

To serve, stand each pear up straight and drizzle with the brown sugar syrup. Serve with the mascarpone, if you like.

SWEET RED MISO POPCORN

SERVES 4 AS A SNACK

2 tbsp red miso
125 g/4½ oz light brown sugar
70 g/2½ oz unsalted butter
1 tsp vegetable oil
100 g/3½ oz popcorn kernels

A must-try for all popcorn lovers. Covered in a tangy red miso sugar, this is your sweet-and-salty popcorn upgrade. The caramel has a dense chew to it, providing pops of intense flavour with every bite.

Pulse-blend the red miso and sugar in a food processor until the mixture resembles wet sand, then warm over a low heat in a heavy-based saucepan until the sugar begins to melt.

Heat a separate, large, heavy-based saucepan with a lid. Melt 20 g/¾ oz of the butter in the pan, then pour in the vegetable oil. Add the corn and stir to coat the kernels thoroughly, then clamp on the lid.

After 3–4 minutes, the corn kernels will begin to pop. It will take a full 8–10 minutes before all the corn is popped.

While the corn is still warm, toss in the rest of the butter. Add the miso sugar 1 tbsp at a time, then, using a small soft spatula, spread it around the popcorn until evenly distributed and all the miso sugar has been used up. This has to be done carefully, since the miso sugar is a little sticky and the popcorn is fragile.

Finally, transfer the popcorn to a flat tray for cooling. Enjoy as soon as it's cool enough not to burn your mouth!

ALMOND AND SWEET WHITE MISO CAKE

MAKES A 20 CM/8 IN CAKE
SERVES 8

---

180 g/6 oz unsalted butter, softened, plus more for the tin
180 g/6 oz self-raising (self-rising) flour, plus more for the tin
150 g/5½ oz caster (superfine) sugar
150 g/5½ oz *saikyo* (sweet white) miso
50 g/1¾ oz ground almonds (almond flour)
3 eggs, lightly beaten
1½ tsp baking powder
75 ml/2½ fl oz full-fat milk
40 g/1½ oz flaked (sliced) almonds

This cake brings back floods of memories from my first ever research trip to Japan almost 16 years ago. I was meeting one of the most prestigious miso-makers in Japan, Ishino Miso. After the privilege of witnessing the annual harvesting of sweet miso, ready for New Year's Eve, I was sent away with a little gift box so elaborate I was too self-conscious to open it in front of everyone.

As soon as I got back to the hotel room, I was beside myself with excitement to discover a big fluffy cake flavoured with the famous *saikyo* miso for which the factory was known. This is a young, sweet white miso with a custardy flavour, which is then whipped into a light sponge cake. I remember the crunch of the almonds along the top as I bit down into meltingly soft-pillow cake.

After many attempts over the years, this is a version of that impossibly fluffy sponge cake. It is so delicious served with a hot, slightly bitter matcha green tea. It really transports me back to those early research trips, when miso was still a mystery to me.

Preheat the oven to 160°C fan/180°C/350°F/gas mark 4. Butter a 20 cm/8 in cake tin (pan), then dust it lightly with flour, tapping to remove the excess.

Cream the butter and the sugar for a few minutes until light and fluffy, scraping down the sides of the bowl if you are using a mixer. Add the miso and ground almonds and beat again until smooth.

Pour in the beaten eggs a little at a time, beating well after each addition. The mixture should be pale and light.

In a separate bowl, sift the flour and baking powder together, then fold into the batter with a spatula. Add the milk slowly until the mixture falls easily off a spoon. Pour the batter into the prepared tin and smooth the top, then sprinkle with the flaked almonds.

Bake for 45–50 minutes on the middle shelf of the oven, until a skewer comes out clean from the centre of the cake. Leave to cool on a wire rack before serving.

MISO CARAMEL 3 WAYS

Thanks largely to TV baking shows, the mighty miso caramel has become a phenomenon over the last decade. Similar to salted caramel, but smoother and deeper in flavour, it is hard to find anyone who does not like it. Over the years, I have perfected my miso caramel recipe so that it is foolproof. Here it is, plus more ideas for how to use it in other desserts.

EASY MISO CARAMEL SAUCE

MAKES ABOUT 1 LITRE/1¾ PINTS

200 g/7 oz caster (superfine) sugar
200 g/7 oz light brown sugar
470 ml/17 fl oz whipping cream
100 g/3½ oz runny honey
70 g/2½ oz unsalted butter
65 g/2¼ oz white miso
¼ tsp sea salt flakes

Heating sugars in a home kitchen is not easy and can often go wrong. There is nothing more frustrating than not nailing caramelization and having to throw all your hard work away. But never fear! My recipe has evolved to become a bit of cheat's caramel, since it comes together in 15 minutes without the need for a sugar thermometer.

Delicious on ice cream, brownies, profiteroles, bananas, sponge cakes… there is little I wouldn't pour this over! Keep it on standby, ready to whip up into impromptu desserts and sweet treats.

Combine both the sugars, the cream, honey and butter in a heavy-based saucepan. Set over a medium heat for about 10 minutes, until the sugars and butter have melted. Reduce the heat to low and continue to simmer, stirring frequently, for a final 5 minutes.

Take the pan off the heat and whisk in the miso and salt at the same time, then pour into a heatproof bowl to cool.

Once the sauce is ready, keep it in a clean, sterilized jar (I usually just wipe a jar with clear alcohol, such as vodka) in the refrigerator. This will keep for up to 10 days and makes a wonderful gift.

MISO CARAMEL 3 WAYS

MISO FUDGE BONBONS

MAKES A 30 X 20 CM/ 12 X 10 IN TRAY

Traditional sweet-shop caramels are getting a glow-up here with umami-rich miso! I love making these to give as gifts. Simply gather all the ingredients for the Easy Miso Caramel recipe (see page 209). Butter a 30 x 20 cm/12 x 10 in baking tray and line it with baking paper (parchment paper), leaving a bit of extra paper around the sides, as you will need it to lift out the bonbons.

Combine both the sugars, the cream, honey and butter in a heavy-based saucepan over a medium heat for about 10 minutes, until the sugars and butter have melted.

Take the pan off the heat and whisk in the miso paste and salt. Return to a low heat and continue to simmer, stirring frequently, for 35 minutes. The caramel will become darker in colour.

Pour into the prepared baking tray and, once cool, transfer to the refrigerator to set. Once set, cut into squares.

To make these more gift-like, cut out small rectangles of baking paper, use them to wrap each bonbon and twist at both ends. Store in an airtight container. These will keep for up to a week at room temperature and up to a month in the refrigerator.

MISO CARAMEL CHOCOLATES

MAKES 16

60 g/2¼ oz good-quality milk chocolate chips
60 g/2¼ oz good-quality dark (bittersweet) chocolate chips
150 g/5½ oz Easy Miso Caramel Sauce (see page 209)

I tried freshly made chocolate caramels at Hawksmoor restaurant in London, which I loved so much that I immediately plotted how miso could make them even better. These make great gifts and are perfect served with a double espresso.

You will need a silicone mould for hemispherical chocolates, and a small paintbrush or pastry brush.

Set a heatproof bowl over a saucepan of simmering water over a medium heat, making sure the bowl does not touch the water. Put both types of chocolate chips into the bowl and melt them. Remove the bowl from the pan to cool. You can also melt the chocolate in a microwave in 25-second bursts, giving it a quick stir between each, until fully melted.

Spoon chocolate into 16 holes of a hemispherical silicone chocolate mould until each is only about one-third full.

Use a clean paintbrush or small pastry brush to paint the chocolate up the sides of each of the hollows. This is to ensure the miso caramel is fully covered in chocolate later. Place the silicone mould in the refrigerator so the chocolate can set. This will take about 20 minutes.

Spoon the miso caramel into the chocolate mould until almost full. Then cover with the remaining chocolate. (If the chocolate is no longer runny, then gently re-melt it so it is runny enough to be spooned.)

Return to the refrigerator and allow to set for at least 30 minutes.

Gently remove the chocolates from the moulds and keep them in an airtight container in the refrigerator, removing at least an hour before serving. Eat within a week... that shouldn't be too hard!

MISO CARAMEL TARTLETS

MAKES SIX 10 CM/4 IN TARTLETS

For the pastry
125 g/4½ oz plain (all-purpose) flour, plus more to dust
55 g/2 oz cold unsalted butter
2–3 tbsp ice-cold water
sea salt

For the caramel filling
200 g/7 oz caster (superfine) sugar
2 tbsp water
100 g/3½ oz unsalted butter, chopped
50 g/1¾ oz white miso
200 ml/7 fl oz double (heavy) cream, plus more to serve

Salty caramels are a great love of mine: sweetness followed by deep saltiness is a wonderful experience for the palate that is close to the flavour of long-fermented, darker misos. These are quick and easy tarts that can be whipped up as a weekend treat. I like to serve with whipped cream for maximum indulgence.

You will need six 10 cm/4 in tartlet tins (pans).

Sift the flour into a large mixing bowl and add a pinch of salt. Cut the cold butter into small cubes and add to the flour. Using your fingertips, rub the butter into the flour, lifting it in the bowl to keep it light and cool. Continue until it resembles crumbs.

Sprinkle with some of the ice-cold water and start to bring the pastry together, picking up any stray pieces and bringing them into the dough. Sprinkle in more water if required.

Place the dough on a work surface sprinkled lightly with flour and knead lightly to form a smooth ball. Divide into 6 even balls. Roll out each ball using a few short strokes to avoid stretching. Give the dough a quarter turn each time you roll, to keep the round shape. Stop when each piece is 12 cm/4½ in in diameter.

Place the tartlet tins on a baking sheet, then lift each piece of pastry over a rolling pin and across each tin. Press the dough into the edges of the tin using your fingers; don't trim the edges yet. Chill for 30 minutes.

Preheat the oven to 170°C fan/190°C/375°F/gas mark 5.

Continues overleaf

Fill each pastry case with rounds of baking paper (parchment paper) and add baking beans or raw rice to weigh it down. Bake for 10 minutes. Remove the paper and beans or rice and cook the pastry for a further 5 minutes. Trim the excess pastry on each tart tin using a small sharp knife, then leave to cool on a wire cooling rack.

Reduce the oven temperature to 140°C fan/160°C/325°F/gas mark 3.

Make the filling: put the sugar and measured water into a large saucepan and heat gently, stirring. When the sugar has completely dissolved, increase the heat until it turns a rich caramel colour. It will bubble and spit if it is too hot, so keep an eye on the heat. Remove from the heat and stir in the butter and miso, followed by the cream. Return to the heat and boil until the sauce is thick enough to leave a gap on the base of the pan when you draw a spoon across it.

Fill the pastry cases with the caramel and return to the oven for 8–10 minutes until the filling is bubbling. Cool for 10 minutes before removing carefully from the tins. Serve with cream.

MISO APPLE CREAM CHEESE CRUMBLE

SERVES 12

150 g/5½ oz unsalted butter, softened, plus more for the baking tin (pan)
500 g/1 lb 2 oz tart apples, such as Braeburn or Granny Smith
25 g/1 oz white miso
4 tbsp maple syrup
175 g/6 oz light brown sugar, plus 1 tbsp
4 eggs
250 g/9 oz plain (all-purpose) flour
1 tsp bicarbonate of soda (baking soda)
165 g/5¾ oz full-fat cream cheese

For the crumble topping
100 g/3½ oz unsalted butter, chopped
150 g/5½ oz plain (all-purpose) flour
30 g/1 oz light brown sugar
1 tsp freshly grated nutmeg

TIP: For two variations, swap the apples with pears or bananas, which also pair well with miso flavours.

A timeless English classic that was begging for a miso twist! Miso and apples are wonderful friends: the sharpness of apple is rounded by the umami of miso just as it is enveloped by a deep caramel flavour too. This traybake has a lovely crumbly topping and pairs well with ice cream, cream or even Miso Custard (see page 200).

Preheat the oven to 180°C fan/200°C/400°F/gas mark 6. Butter a 30 x 23 cm/12 x 9½ in baking tin (pan) with baking paper (parchment paper).

In a large bowl, rub together all the crumble topping ingredients until you have even crumbs, then put in the refrigerator to chill.

Peel and core the apples and slice into wedges.

In a small bowl, mix together the miso, maple syrup and the 1 tbsp of sugar, then transfer to a small saucepan and warm through until runny. Set aside.

In a large bowl, beat the 175 g/6 oz light brown sugar, the butter, eggs, flour, bicarb and 65 g/2½ oz of the cream cheese with electric beaters, until the whole mixture is pale and smooth. Fold the apples into the creamy mix and pour into the tin.

Get the crumble from the refrigerator and scatter it in a layer on top of the creamy mix. Add the rest of the cream cheese in blobs, dotting them around the tin. Drizzle over about 3 tbsp of the miso maple syrup across the top, reserving the rest.

Bake for 35 minutes, then leave to cool in the tin, drizzling over the rest of the miso maple syrup to finish.

This will keep in an airtight container for 3–4 days.

INDEX

DEDICATION

This book is dedicated to my grandma, who lived to 100 and passed away a week before I finished writing it. In her final decade, she always drank from a Miso Tasty cup.

ACKNOWLEDGEMENTS

To do one thing well has long been a philosophy of mine.

Making miso my *raison d'être* for the last 15 years, however, was not easy. For a long time, I was criticized for choosing something far too niche. I was told that it would be impossible to forge a career from 'just' miso. There was definitely some truth in that: the early years were a fight for survival, until miso became popular. As I look back now, I really believe I backed the right horse: by focussing on doing one thing well, my job was well done.

I wrote this book during an extraordinary time for me. The deadline for handing in the manuscript coincided neatly with my final week at the miso company I founded 15 years ago, Miso Tasty, a global retail brand of miso products. I have left Miso Tasty and my team in their new home, Belazu, a food company I have long admired, though I remain an advisor to the business. The synchronicity of writing this book over the last 12 months, together with the handing over of my miso business, has made this project particularly cathartic and meaningful.

My aim was to create and update the only miso cookbook you will ever need. This book truly contains everything I have ever learnt about miso from more than a decade of specializing in a single ingredient. I hope that everything in this book remains evergreen. I am really proud of it.

I would like to thank the amazing team at Pavilion Books. Thanks to commissioning editor Lucy Smith and publishing and design director Laura Russell for trusting me in my vision. A big thank you to Alice Kennedy-Owen for jumping on the miso train so enthusiastically and making it a beautiful modern classic, while respecting its origins. Thank you to Emily Preece-Morrison who commissioned the original edition. Always grateful to Lucy B for editing each of my cookbooks with her beady eyes. Thank you also to my lovely agents Charlie Campbell and Fiona Smith, for representing my writing and for believing in me from day one.

This beautiful book, with its stunning cover, would have been impossible without the genius styling of my wonderful and incredibly talented friend Aya Nishimura or the visionary photography of Yuki Sugiura. I have had so much fun working with you both and it is truly an honour to collaborate again with you both on *our* miso book! Thank you for your friendship.

Many thanks to Clare Owen for the lush illustrations for this edition of the cookbook – you have brought a real warmth to the food science and stories here, tying it all together beautifully.

Malcolm, I have long felt guilty for taking credit for your genius, and I am about to do it all again with this book. Thank you for contributing so much of the science and deep thinking for MISO. Malcolm is the original under-appreciated and often-misunderstood partner in Miso Tasty.

There are so many Miso Tasty ninjas that I would like to acknowledge. I can't name you all, but thanks to Hannah, Jimmy, Floss, Ellie, Clare, Jess, Chloe, Dora, Chris, Paul, Sam, Rhona, Rebecca R and your uncle David R, Philip Numbers Newlyn, Chris B, Sue, and the superwoman that is Nadine LB. Thank you for being my friend.

David Balmer and Monica Turner of WJFG deserve a special thank you for changing the course of Miso Tasty and, indeed, my life forever. Shout out to all the new disciples of Miso at Belazu, including my homies Vix, Katie K, Ash, Claudia, Taryn, Sarah D, Dani and Rory for continuing to fly the Miso Tasty flag. Thank you also to Graham and Liz for always looking after me in Australia. I appreciate you all; thank you for taking care of my Miso Tasty baby.

Thank you to Mr Hayashi for opening the world of miso to me and keeping the door open for others. Big love to Kie Kajihara for being my first miso fixer and travel companion. Thank you to Shoki Shiozawa for drinking with me and being my friend through it all. Shout out to Keiji san for being the flint in this crazy journey. Heartfelt thanks to Sunho and the whole Noda family who opened their home and hearts to my curiosity for traditional miso-making: *arigato gozaimasu*!

I would like to thank all the investors who supported Miso Tasty on its journey. You will always have my heart for believing in me and my dream. I think of you often. Forgive mi-so.

To my family, who are there for me, more than I realize.

To Merlin, my best friend since we were 11. Thank you for always being here for me both before and after this mighty miso chapter and for always adding miso to your potatoes.

To Noah, my champion. Miso Mouse waves and bows out.

Miso miss you already.

Bonnie x